The System of Nature in the 21st Century

A Book About Truth & Knowledge

By
Bob Almada

The System of Nature in the 21st Century
Copyright © 2021 by *Bob Almada*

All rights reserved. No part of this publication may be reproduced, distributed, or transmitted in any form or by any means, including photocopying, recording, or other electronic or mechanical methods, without the prior written permission of the author, except in the case of brief quotations embodied in critical reviews and certain other non-commercial uses permitted by copyright law.

ISBN
978-1-954932-73-9 (Paperback)
978-1-954932-72-2 (eBook)

Dedication

This book is dedicated to

Paul Henri Thierry

The original author of

The System of Nature

Table of Contents

Dedication — iii
PREFACE — vii

CHAPTER I
Nature and Her Laws — 3

CHAPTER II
Motion and Its Origin — 11

CHAPTER III
Matter and Its Various Combinations;
The Course of Nature — 19

CHAPTER IV
Laws of Motion; Attraction and Repulsion;
Inert Force; Necessity — 23

CHAPTER V
Order and Confusion; Intelligence; Chance — 31

CHAPTER VI
Moral and Physical Distinctions; Origins — 39

CHAPTER VII
The Soul and The Spiritual System — 47

CHAPTER VIII
Intellectual Faculties Derived From The Faculty of Feeling — 57

CHAPTER IX
Diversity of The Intellectual Faculties;
Physical Causes and Moral Qualities;
The Natural Principles of Society; Morals; Politics — 67

CHAPTER X
The Soul — 89

The System of Nature

VOLUME 1

CHAPTER XI
The System of Our Free Agency   105

CHAPTER XII
Is The System of Fatalism Dangerous?   125

CHAPTER XIII
The Immortality of the Soul; The Doctrine of a Future State;
The Fear of Death   145

CHAPTER XIV
Education, Morals, and Laws Suffice to Restrain Us;
The Desire of Immortality; Suicide   165

CHAPTER XV
Our True Interest = Our Happiness;
We Cannot Be Happy Without Virtue   177

CHAPTER XVI
Errors; What Constitutes Happiness;
The True Source of Evil   191

CHAPTER XVII
Remedies For Our Evils; Recapitulation   203

CONCLUSION   209

Preface

The source of the problems that plague the world we live in is our ignorance of Nature. We blindly embrace the lessons of our childhood and develop prejudices that warp our minds. We cannot grow as long as we accept fiction as truth. We are like a child who believes what adults tell us even if they are wrong. To change this we must be willing to examine our beliefs with open minds. We must be able to differentiate truth from fiction. Too frequently errors push truth to the side and we base our beliefs and actions on false ideas. We need to base our actions and beliefs on factual information. Indeed, we have created imaginary worlds where happiness and misery are paramount. We ignore reality and meditate on figments of the imagination. We neglect our experiences and instead rely on speculation and indulge in guessing on how to obtain happiness. Our most important job is to rid ourselves of belief in myths and delusions that will only lead us astray. The answers are in Nature! Only in Nature will we find the antidotes to our misunderstandings of the world in which we live. Truth is unwavering and necessary if we are to grow. The truth will never harm us! When error is presented as truth it becomes a tool for those who want power that is gained through the ignorance of the masses. Many politicians and religious leaders obtain power through repeated lies. The majority of people in most countries are subjected to poverty which is a form of slavery to the wealthy, the corporations, the politicians, and religious leaders. Priests were the first to control large groups of people through lies about fanciful all powerful beings. They successfully instilled fear into the lives of common people. Acts of hatred, barbarous persecutions, and numerous massacres can be traced back to religious beliefs. These beliefs result in ignorance of the truths of Nature, the understanding of which would lead to actions beneficial to all. The aforementioned powerful don't want common people to experience nature and truth because such knowledge would set them free.

Our goal should be to seek out the truth and eliminate anything that gets in the way of progress toward individual happiness and a civilized society. Within a civilized society we will have the courage to respect reason and seek out the truth. We will rely on experience and not be subject to an imagination which was programmed with lies by authority figures. In doing so we will let go of the prejudices we learned as children. Morals will be based on our nature, our wants, and the needs of the society within which we live. We will dare to love ourselves and pursue happiness by promoting that of others. When we let go of false beliefs that are useless and dangerous, we will become virtuous and rational beings which will result in personal happiness. And if we must have our superstitious beliefs, at least let others form their beliefs in their own manner, since nothing can be more immaterial than thinking about ideas or beings that are not subject to reason. One's beliefs should not be harmful to others. We should all believe that it is of the utmost importance to be JUST, KIND, and PEACEFUL. The goals of the following pages are to restore the temple of truth and to build an altar whose foundation is morality, reason, and justice. When virtue is guarded by truth and clothed in experience we the people will be the beneficiaries. We will start a new era where the accepted truth is the belief that happiness is the goal of our existence which can only be obtained BY PROMOTING THAT OF OUR FELLOW CREATURES.

> *In short, we should learn to know, that happiness is simply a quality that emanates and is formed by reflection. As such, we should each be the sun of our own system, continually shedding around genial rays. In turn we will keep our own existence constantly supplied with the required energy to put forth kindly fruit.*

Part 1

**Laws of Nature and of Humans
The faculties of the soul
The doctrine of imortality
Happiness**

Chapter 1

Nature and Her Laws

We deceive ourselves when we abandon experience to believe in imaginary systems. We are created by nature, exist in nature, and adhere to the laws of nature. Even our thoughts are controlled by nature. We cannot escape this reality. Beings that are "above nature" are illusions we have created based on what we have seen and experienced, yet which we can never fully complete with regards to the beings place of existence or it's manner of acting. There can be nothing outside of Nature that includes other beings. Therefore, instead of looking to supreme beings for happiness we should study Nature. We must learn her laws, understand her forces, observe the unchallengeable rules by which she works, and apply them to our existence in order to secure our own happiness. Accept the things in nature that we do not understand as simply that. Know that we are always governed by the laws of nature whether we understand them or not.

The idea that the physical being and the moral being are different is incorrect. We are purely physical beings. The moral being is the physical being acting as we do based on the way we think. The way we think is the work of Nature! Our visible actions as well as our internal actions, both of which are controlled by Nature, combine to make the physical being. We are also influenced by our surroundings. All these factors combine to make us who we are, which is beings in search of happiness. All that we do, think, are, and will be is nothing more than what Universal Nature has made us. Our ideas, our actions, and our will are the necessary effects of properties given to us by Nature and combined with the circumstances within which we exist. We are part of the masterpiece which is Nature acting with the tools she has created.

We are born into this world naked and needy. We learn to cover our nakedness and find shelter. Our earliest ancestors used the skins of beasts and built artless huts. By degrees we improved the quality of our cloths and our shelters. Soon we were taking clay, gold, and fossils from the earth to continuously improve the quality of our existence. Although the quality of life improved as civilized societies developed, we were always subject to the laws of nature. The steps taken to control our existence should be viewed as a long succession of causes and effects, which are nothing more than the development of the first impulses given to us by nature. Indeed, we see an animal pass from simple to complex wants as part of its nature. The butterfly starts as an egg which produces a worm which forms a cocoon which becomes the most beautiful of insects. At this stage it reproduces and dies completing nature's cycle for this species. We see the same cycle in the world of vegetables and flowers. It is the same for us. All of the motions and changes we experience are a function of the laws that govern our organization and the matter of which we are composed.

The *physical being* is one who acts with motives that we are able to comprehend.

The *moral being* acts in a physical way, with some degree of self-control.

The *wild being* acts like a child without experience who is incapable of creating happiness due to not having learned how to resist impulses from exterior beings.

The *civilized being* has learned from personal and social experiences how to draw from nature to create happiness and resist impulses from exterior beings when experience has shown that they would be destructive.

The *enlightened being* is mature and striving for perfection. We are capable of creating our own happiness because we have learned to think for ourselves and not formulate opinions based on what others are telling us is the truth. We know from experience that critical investigations often prove the aforementioned truths to be false.

The *happy being* knows how to enjoy nature's bounty. We think for ourselves; we are thankful for what we have; we do not envy the welfare of others; and we do not long for imaginary benefits that are always out of our reach.

The *unhappy being* is not able to enjoy the benefits of nature. Such people allow others to think for them; they ignore the good they possess, always looking for ideal benefits that they will never find; they are always in search of that which does not exist.

As a result we should always try to learn from our experiences and from our understanding of natural philosophy. Our ideas about religions, morals, legislation, political governments, arts, sciences, pleasures, and most importantly, our misfortunes, should be based on our experiences and natural philosophies. Through experience we see that Nature acts by simple, regular, and unchanging laws. Through the senses we are bound to this Universal Nature and must learn from experience about her laws. Through our perceptions we must discover her secrets. When we ignore our experiences or gives up on understanding them, we stumble into the abyss and the imagination leads us off course. Such mistakes are physical.

We deceive ourselves when we fail to go back to nature, look to her laws, and call on practical knowledge to guide us. Because we do not have practical knowledge we form imperfect ideas about matter and its properties, combinations, powers, energies, and modes of action. As such, our views of the world and the universe are incorrect. We view ordinary occurrences as miraculous. We wonder at everything and understand nothing. The people that we allow to guide us are most interested in taking advantage of us. Because we are ignorant of nature and have mistaken her laws, we do not know how to find our own happiness within her.

By not understanding the laws of nature, we do not understand ourselves. The consequence is that our beliefs, ideas, and ability to reason become nothing more than a long chain of errors, all because experience plays no role in their development. Error is never beneficial. Because of our own self-deception the human race is plunged into misery. Because we neglect nature and do not understand her laws, we create Gods of the most ridiculous and preposterous form. These Gods become the sole object of our hopes and fears. Unhappy humans tremble under the influence of these visionary deities, creatures that we created. We feared blocks of stone or burning logs or flying fish or other beings that were thought to have powers above those of nature. The powers that such objects or beings possess can only be created in the minds of humans. How interesting that we can look back and see the absurdity of ancient religions. Indeed, the ancient mythology with all the petty and absurd attributes attached to it by ignorance is now viewed as laughable.

Nature distributes equally her wonders and her misfortunes. She does so without forethought and malice, but only follows her absolute laws, when she creates being or destroys them; when she causes good people to suffer; when she scatters among decent people good and evil; and when she subjects all of us to constant change. We were not able to embrace Nature and look for solutions to our problems, pains, deficiencies, and happiness within her. Instead we created fantastic beings that were and still are above Nature. We made them the authors of our joys and sorrows.

Because of our ignorance of Nature we created illusive powers that cause us to tremble with fear and require superstitious worship. These beliefs have been the source of misery and the evils handed down to future generations. Because we have not been able to see our own nature and determine the proper course of actions as they relate to our wants and rights, people in most societies have fallen from FREEDOM to SLAVERY! Either we have forgotten the purpose of our existence or we forced ourselves to subdue the natural desires of the heart. We sacrifice our welfare to the whims of leaders that we have elected or that we submit to without examination. We did not, and do not, understand that the true nature of submitting to leaders and governments are guarantees of protection and happiness. The goal of all governments should be the well-being of the governed and not the interests of the governors.

In the world we currently live in the governors are the corporations, the wealthy, and the politicians. We give into these powers without thought and awareness. They want us to believe that they are superior beings, Gods here on earth, so they can profit from our ignorance and take advantage of our misguided views. They work to corrupt us and render us vicious by enslaving us and making us miserable. Human beings were intended by Nature to enjoy liberty as a result of their experiences with her laws and secrets. Instead we have fallen into servitude to bad governments, bad corporations, and religions. We lost sight of how to attain our own happiness and thus the happiness of others. We do not know how to treat ourselves, what excesses to avoid, what desires to resist, or what impulses to follow in order to promote our own well-being. Ignorance of our true interests has led us to submit to living with irregularities, excesses, shameful extravagance, and a long train of vices, at the expense of our preservation and leading to the loss of our enduring prosperity.

Ignorance of ourselves has kept us from discovering morals that would benefit our societies. Corrupt powers that control us want us to remain ignorant. Indeed, over time, the influence of ignorance aided by corruption has enfeebled the voice of the common individual. As such we will never know the truth and always be at odds with our fellow beings. Our ignorance has lasted so long because we neglect to study the laws of nature. Instead we allow ourselves to be led by example, routine, and the authority of others. As such, we avoid change and cling to a uniformed respect for ancient ideas. We hang on to the most absurd and ridiculous institutions handed down from generation to generation. We fear changes that would improve our condition, and even view such ideas as irreverent. Rather than be led by example we must follow our experience which will demand action. Rather than be subject to routine we must be guided by reason which will require reflection. As opposed to being told the "truth" by authorities we must indulge in diligent and patient investigation. We will only benefit when we listen to those trying to show us the dangers of traveling the road away from common sense and Nature.

Nations with the most shameful of histories have never learned this lesson. Progress in medicine, natural philosophy, agriculture, the arts, and all useful sciences have been controlled and hindered by authority for centuries. They prefer wild imaginings and mindless conjectures to the scientific endeavors and labored experience that has and will continue to expose the secrets of nature. Unfortunately, either laziness or terror or both have negated common sense. Beliefs and actions are guided by imagination, excitement, habit, preconceived opinions, and above all, by the influence of authority. People who are hungry for power and who know how to deceive, turn ignorance into approval and take advantage of laziness. Thus imaginary and unsubstantiated systems have taken the place of experience, mature reflection, and reason. Petrified by fear, intoxicated with the marvelous, and stupefied by laziness, we give up on learning from our experiences. As such, we become inexperienced which leads to beliefs in vague fantasies and the formation of the most ridiculous opinions. And where did these harmful ideas come from? Those idle notions are pushed by authority figures who are interested in keeping the masses in a sad state of ignorance.

The human race remains in a state of infancy because we do not pay attention to Nature and her ways. We do not use our ability to reason. We allow ourselves to be controlled by the unbelievable and the supernatural. As a result of these failings we are in constant fear. We TREMBLE! For these reasons we cannot grow from a child to an adult. We hold the most trivial theories as sacred truths which we are not permitted to doubt or challenge, not even for an instant. Our ignorance made us gullible, our curiosity made us believe the unbelievable, and over time our misguided perceptions became our realities. These beliefs were passed on from race to race as truths. Tyrannical powers supported these false beliefs because it was through them that they could enslave an entire society. From time to time Nature would project a beacon of light into the darkness, and some would embrace it, but the ignorance of the many combined with their love of the marvelous smothered the momentary flame. The masses were first deceived by their own gullibility, and then they were forced into submission. The science of humans became a confused mass of darkness, falsehoods, and contradictions. A ray of truth furnished by Nature will always be present to some degree. Our perceptions and necessities will continuously bring us back to Nature. As such, our goals should be to raise ourselves above the mythical notions that have possessed us for so long. We must be able to look at our beliefs and our societies and analyze them with open minds. Only then can we learn to challenge those chaotic origins that have held us back. We must learn to allow our experiences to guide us. We will find ourselves looking into Nature, examining her laws, and studying her as deeply as possible to formulate our ideas about the beings that exist within her bounty. We've been taught that the common sense and reason that would lead us to the truth about our existence are not to be trusted. As we examine and grow to understand the visible world, belief in an invisible world will no longer have a place in an intellectual world. In this world, reason and common sense will be valued, encouraged, and nurtured.

Within the universe, that vast assemblage of everything that exists, we see only matter and motion. As we study them we see an uninterrupted succession of causes and effects. Some causes are known to us because we experience them immediately or over long periods of time. Others are unknown to us because their effects are not easily observed. A vast range of matter, combined under infinitely many forms, constantly communicates by sending and receiving impulses. The different qualities of matter, its countless combinations, and its modes of action are the consequences of these associations. We refer to these associations as the ESSENCE of beings. From these essences comes the order, classes, or systems which these beings respectively possess. The sum total is known by the term nature.

Nature is the great whole that consists of matter under its various combinations with a variety of motions that we can experience. Nature in each individual being is the different qualities, the combinations, the impulses, and the various modes of action that differentiate beings. Thus, OUR nature is the result of certain combinations of matter that have different properties that give and receive certain impulses. This arrangement is called organization which is our ability to feel, think, act, and move in a manner that distinguishes us from other comparable beings. We rank in an order, in a system, and in a class by ourselves. We are different from other animals that do not possess the properties that we possess. The different systems of beings, which is the particular nature of each being, depends on the general system of the great whole that is the Universal Nature of which they are part. Every being is necessarily attached to that Universal Nature. To be clear, the purpose here is to define the term NATURE. There is no intent to personify nature when talking about it producing particular effects. All effects are the result of particular properties that make up the greater whole. For example, when considering the phrase 'Nature demands that we pursue happiness,' it should be understood that a property of a being that thinks, feels, and acts is to work toward its own happiness. It's natural for a being to seek out that which contributes to its existence and accept that which is part of the cycle of nature. Health is natural to us in a certain state; disease is part of another; and death yet another. The ESSENCE of a being is that of its current state. The essence of a being is its particular individual nature.

Chapter 2

Motion and Its Origin

Motion is an effect by which a body changes its position in space, relative to its distance from other bodies. Motion establishes a relation between our senses and exterior and interior beings. Due to motion we know that beings exist. We can judge their properties, distinguish different kinds of beings, and classify them. The beings we are referring to are the effects of a certain combination of causes, which become causes in their turn. A CAUSE is a being that puts another in motion and produces some change in it. The EFFECT is the change produced in one body, by the motion or presence of another. The essence of a being is its ability to produce, receive and communicate through a variety of motions. Some beings affect our organs and bring about changes in those organs. Beings which do not move us or give us ideas cannot be known to us. To see is to have an object act on and move our visual organs. To hear is the result of movement in our auditory nerves. In short, we have no knowledge of a body or an object until we receive impulses from it.

Nature is the collection of all beings, some that we know of and some that we have not experienced. The continuous action and re-action of these beings results in a series of causes and effects. The laws that govern a being cause it to move or act in a determined manner. When we don't know what constitutes the essence of a being, it's because we don't understand the principles that guide its motion. When we experience something we don't understand we must conclude that it's the result of elements or bodies whose modes of action, impulses, or different effects are not known to us.

We observe two kinds of motion. One is a motion that we experience immediately like a stone falling or a ball rolling or an arm moving. The other is an internal or concealed motion. This is the essence of the being which is the movement of very small particles of matter that result in changes to the larger being. The motion of the particles in flour can be combined to make bread. We see the results of this kind of motion in plants and animals and in humans, as each grows and gets stronger. In humans the internal motion that takes place is called INTELLECTUAL FACULTIES, THOUGHTS, and PASSIONS or the will. These we can only judge by the actions they create. When we see someone running away we judge that person to be interiorly moved to action by the passion of fear. Motion, whether visible or not, is referred to as ACQUIRED when it is impressed on one body by another. It can be a cause that we are not familiar with or one which we can detect. An example of *acquired motion* is the motion that the wind gives to the sails of a ship. That kind of motion is also referred to as SPONTANEOUS since it acts or moves by its own peculiar energy. A person who walks, talks, and thinks displays this kind of motion as well. None the less, upon closer examination we must conclude that there is no such thing as spontaneous motion in any of the different bodies of Nature. Because these bodies are constantly acting upon one another, their changes can be attributed to causes that we can either see or not see. Our will is moved by an exterior cause that we are not aware of, yet it produces changes in us.

SIMPLE MOTION is when a body is put into motion by a single cause. When a body is put into motion by two or more causes, that are equal or unequal, working separately or together, and that are known or unknown, it is referred to as COMPOUND MOTION. Motion is the necessary consequence of the essence of a being. Recall that the essences of beings are the properties that drive them to action. As such each being can only move in a particular manner that conforms to its specific energies and those bodies from which it receives impulses. This is the invariable law of motion. It is *invariable* because it can never change without producing chaos in the essence of things. So a heavy body must fall as long as nothing gets in the way. Similarly, a sensible body must naturally seek pleasure and avoid pain. A fire must burn and emit light. All beings follow a natural path unless a greater cause interrupts that path. Fire will burn until it is doused with water. A sensible being stops seeking pleasure as soon as there is a fear that pain will be the result. Communication of motion depends on the conformity that exists between beings. Fire will only start when there is matter that will burn.

Because the essence of matter is to act, everything in the universe is in motion. Bodies that appear to be at rest are in a state of constant motion that cannot be seen. All beings are constantly breeding, increasing, decreasing, or dispersing either quickly or slowly. The insect called the EPHEMERON, which is born and dies on the same day, experiences rapid changes that can be observed. A hard stone, which appears to be motionless, is changed by the motion of air. A piece of iron is dissolved as rust eats away at it. The aromas that we sense means that there is motion coming from a body that appears to be still. The motion of light allows us to see the stars. Observation and reflection should convince us that everything in Nature is in a continuous state of motion. Not a single part, no matter how small, is ever at rest. Without motion, Nature would cease to exist. When asked the question, "Where did Nature and her continuous motion come from?" the reply from science is it all began with "The Big Bang". Before that the answer is that we do not know. No one knows. We may never know. All we have is that matter is in constant motion and Nature consists of matter in a wide range of different forms.

There are people who choose to ignore what they observe in Nature and explain forms of motion that they do not understand with supreme exterior beings of which they have poorly formed ideas. These people cling to whimsical ideas about our planet and our universe in spite of what science tells us. They observe the effects of gravity and motion yet ignore the fact that matter moves according to the laws of Nature. They could see that when bodies are mixed, in certain situations, motion results, sometimes in surprising ways. For example, iron, Sulfur and water when mixed will heat and ultimately produce a violent explosion. If flour and water are mixed, after a period of time microscopic living beings are formed. As such, inanimate matter can appear to come to life. Is it possible that we came to be as a result of different combinations of matter? Obviously, fermentation and decaying substances produce living beings. The main idea here is that with proper materials newly formed bodies can always be brought into action. The belief that Nature is *uncertain* is held by those who do not reflect and attentively observe her operations.

The energy of motion in matter is seen everywhere, especially when fire, air, and water are combined. Nature combines these elements to create thunder, volcanoes, and earthquakes. Science has shown us the astonishing force generated by combining gunpowder and fire, or the combinations required to create atomic and nuclear bombs. The most terrible effects result when combining matter that is generally believed to be dead and motionless. We can see that motion is produced, developed, and accelerated in matter without the help of an exterior agent. As such, it is reasonable to conclude that motion is the result of the properties existing in different elements and the various combinations of these elements. We've observed many of these combinations and we can also conclude that there are many, infinitely many, that we have not observed. We can also conclude that the effects we are observing require no special agents or supreme beings, who are always more difficult to understand than the effects for which we are giving them credit. If we had paid attention to our observations of Nature, we would not have had the need to create a power outside of Nature. If Nature was a compilation of dead matter that magically came to life, then it would make sense to want to know the source of this motion. But when we view Nature as a whole with infinitely many parts, each with their own properties, that interact with each other in infinitely many ways, then we can conclude that there is no need for supernatural powers. The actions and reactions that occur within the cycle of Nature is an ongoing process and are its own creator and destroyer. If you believe an outside source created matter then you must believe that that source created the motion that is inherent in matter. You must also believe that matter began to exist at some moment in time. This conjecture has never been satisfactorily demonstrated. The CREATION of something from nothing cannot give us any idea of how the universe came into being. This idea gives the mind nothing to examine or work with. The human mind knows only existence and is not capable of conceiving a moment of non-existence. We are not capable of acknowledging the existence of anything that we have not experienced through our senses. We may agree to believe this something exists because we are told it does, but we do so without any form of validation. What moral good can come from blind assurances? This kind of thinking is not consistent with sound doctrine, philosophy, and reason. If someone who claims to be an intellect fails time and time again to prove a hypothesis, would you still accept it as truth? What moral reliance should we give to these people? New ideas will replace old ideas and new systems will take the place of the old. Other Galileo's may be condemned to death and other Newton's may arise. We may reason, argue, dispute, punish, destroy, and even exterminate those whose opinions are different than ours. When all this is done, we will still have to admit that we don't understand how matter came to be or where it got its motion.

Things that we cannot experience with our senses cannot exist for us. There will always be doubts about the things we believe exist that we cannot experience. All free thinkers agree with the position that *nothing can be made from nothing*. Many theologians recognize Nature as an active whole. Most ancient philosophers regarded the world as eternal as is seen by a statement like; *the world has always been and always will be*. Even in the bible, in Genesis it says *"when God made heaven and earth, matter was without form."* If this is true then we must conclude that the world was created from something. The bible never states that the world was made from nothing. And although it does imply a beginning, it absolutely denies an end. *"As it was in the beginning, is now, and ever shall be, world without end."* As such, if matter will never cease to exist, how can one assume it had a beginning? It becomes even harder to understand when you acknowledge that the creator has no extent or parts. How can He create motion as we understand it, which is the change of one body relative to another in space?

It is reasonable to conclude that matter has always existed. It acts and moves according to the essence and energy that each form of matter exhibits individually and in combination with other forms of matter. Anything that exists has specific properties. When bodies interact they will either attract or repel based on the properties they exhibit. Motion within matter determines its properties. Matter without motion and properties are nothing. As soon as matter exists it must act. If it cannot begin to exist, it must have always existed and will never cease to exist. Motion is a manner of being that gives matter its properties and its form of existence. The existence of matter is a fact. The existence of motion is another fact. We observe matter in a variety of forms. So much so that even beings of the same species are never exactly alike. As such, the wide range of matter and motions combine to make infinitely many forms. On the earth we have fire, water, and air which are constantly acting and interacting with each other. Forms of matter are constantly acting, reacting, combining, separating, attracting, and repelling in a cycle of existence that had no beginning and will never end. Nature is an immense chain of causes and effects which continuously flow from each other. The motion of a being is constantly strengthened or weakened, accelerated or retarded, simplified or complicated, procreated or destroyed by the wide range of combinations and circumstances it experiences. If matter were to combine to form a unique and single mass, as some philosophers believe is the case, all would cease to exist. To understand the origins of motion in matter is difficult. We can only speculate about the causes for the motion that gives matter its unique properties. We should be content to base our beliefs on our experiences. The beliefs that *matter always existed; that it moves by virtue of its essence; that all the phenomena of Nature is ascribable to the diversified motion of the variety of matter she contains; and which, like the phoenix, is continually regenerating out of its own ashes.*

Chapter 3

Matter and Its Various Combinations; The Course of Nature

We know some properties of matter because of the effects we can see and experience. We observe range, movement, divisibility, firmness, enormity, and passive force. From these properties we see others like mass, figure, color, etc. So, we give matter properties by the way it affects our senses. Matter should be thought of as a *genus* of beings with some common properties and other properties that make them quite different. Properties common to all matter are magnitude, divisibility, thickness, character, and mobility. Fire has all these properties along with that of producing heat and light. Iron also has all the properties of matter yet when combined with fire it too produces heat and light. These are the necessary results that occur within matter and motion. All the various combinations within Nature are the result of motion and only motion. Through motion everything that exists is created, changes, expands, and is destroyed. Motion changes beings by adding to or taking away their properties which causes them to move from one state to another. These changes contribute to the generation, maintenance, and decomposition of other beings that are completely different in their size and purpose.

Some say the THREE ORDERS OF NATURE are *minerals, vegetables* and *animals*. At certain points in time each uses matter from the other in the course of their life cycles. In all this we see nothing but the effects of motion as each is guided, modified, accelerated or slowed down, and strengthened or weakened, as a result of the properties of each being as they grow and age. Within the existence of each we see continuous change in essence, properties, energies, mass, and qualities. After an animal is born it grows in size and strength. It gets sustenance from plants, other animals, air, water, fire, and the earth itself. When there is a good balance within the animal of all these sustaining factors it has more energy. It acts, thinks, and moves in a different way. It is happy, courageous, and able to exercise its body more easily. It's clear that these elements, the primitive parts of matter, when variously combined are, as a result of continuous motion, assimilated with and provide substance to the animal. The motion of these forms of matter, whether seen or unseen, results in visible changes in a beings shape and actions. Just as these elements can serve to nourish and strengthen a being, they can also serve to weaken and destroy the being. Water, fire, air, and various forms of nourishment, when experienced disproportionately, can cause harm and even result in death.

Plants which serve as a form of nourishment to animals are themselves nourished by the earth. They grow because of the air, water, and matter which they assimilate via their roots and pores. Corn gets its nourishment from the earth and in turn provides nourishment to humans and other animals. The same elements and principles are found in the formation of minerals. Although more dense, they are still broken down by water, fire, and air. Animals, plants, and minerals always give back to Nature. That is to say, they return to basic forms of matter to be used again and again by Nature in an infinite cycle of creation and destruction. When an animal dies, it dissolves, disunites and disperses only to assume new activity and form new combinations which serve to nourish and preserve or destroy other beings. This is the constant and invariable cycle of Nature and living beings. It is motion that creates and preserves for a time and successively destroys one part of the universe by the other. All the while the sum of existence remains eternally the same. Nature creates suns and planets that revolve around them with erratic and continuous motions. When these bodies disperse human beings will have had only the slightest understanding of their existence.

Clearly, it is motion in matter that changes and destroys all beings. Be it a stone, a planet, or an animal, all are subject to the laws of Nature and the changes that result from constant motion within matter. Living beings are born of the dead and the dead come from the living. This is the constant routine of Nature. Who knows, if to live, be not to die, and if to die be not to live? It has been said, "There is neither birth nor death for any mortal, but only a combining and separating of that which was combined. Among mortals these are referred to as birth and death. Only infants or dumb people imagine things are born which did not exist before or that anything can die or perish totally."

Chapter 4

Laws of Motion; Attraction and Repulsion; Inert Force; Necessity

Most people are not surprised by common occurrences they observe like a falling stone. Whenever we see a cause that we understand, its effect does not surprise us. It is only the philosopher, like NEWTON, who wonders why an object falls or behaves as it does. In many cases the simplest of motions are difficult to understand or completely unexplainable. When observing an action that is not common to our senses, we feel the need to understand and explain it. When we see something we don't understand and it seems to present a danger to our well-being, we work hard to understand it. When we are not capable of understanding it, we resort to our imaginations. We become alarmed, fearful, and suspicious. We create fictitious causes for those things that frighten us the most.

Thus our religious error came to be due to things we saw and experienced in Nature that were threatening and that we did not have the capacity to understand. Knowing that Nature follows constant and necessary laws we must be diligent in trying to understand her causes and effects. When we experience something we don't understand, rather than label it as SUPER-NATURAL we must work harder to find the cause or admit that there are some things we are not capable of explaining. Identifying causes with phantoms, fictions, or imaginary beings only takes us further down the road of ignorance and continuous error.

Within Nature a body moves in a simple manner following general laws unless acted upon by causes that change or prevent its mode of action. Our actions have a tendency to make us happy unless we are moved by a cause that opposes natural tendencies. When actions are self-destructive we have been deceived to believe that such actions will result in our happiness, or we have no idea where our actions will lead us. If the motions of a being were always simple it would be easy to predict that beings actions. When a stone is falling it's easy to predict its path unless other forces come into play. Even so, as is the case with most complex motion, it is the result of a combination of simple motions. Therefore, with any complex motion, if we break it down and analyze each part in order we will see a series of simple motions that we understand and expect. So it is clear that simple motion causes different forms of matter to combine and form a wide range of bodies. The whole body is the sum total of each particular motion that combines to make it. Some forms of matter are able to unite with others forming strong and durable bonds. Such bodies are called SOLIDS and consist of a large number of homogeneous, similar and analogous particles. These particles rely on each other for the solid to exist. Similarly, primitive beings have a need for support and the presence of others in order to preserve themselves and acquire their own form of consistency and solidity. This is a truth that applies equally to both our *physical* and the *moral* nature.

The modes of action when observed in matter and bodies are referred to as *attraction, repulsion, sympathy, antipathy, affinities,* and *relations*. Moralist describes these modes of action with terms like *love, hatred, friendship,* and *aversion*. Humans, like all beings in nature, experience the impulses of attraction and repulsion. Unlike other beings in nature, the cause of these impulses is not always obvious. The system of attraction and repulsion is ancient. The love that the ancients describe as leading to chaos is nothing more than a personification of the law of attraction. Their stories about chaos are really about the union of common forms of matter that resulted in the creation of the universe. Discord or repulsion was the cause of dissolution, confusion, and disorder. There is no doubt that this was the origin of TWO PRINCIPLES. The ancients asserted that *"there is a kind of affection by which the elements unite themselves; and a sort of discord, by which they separate or remove themselves."* We know that certain bodies easily unite while others cannot. Water combines easily with salt but not at all with oil. Yet the three can be combined in the right proportions to make soap. Other bonds, like those seen in metals, are quite strong. So matter and its wide range of combinations and proportions result in an almost infinite number of physical and moral bodies. The motion of these bodies is more or less complex implying that some motions are easily understood while others are far more difficult to interpret.

Particles of matter that we cannot see unite with particles they have an attraction with to form bodies that we can see. These bodies unite with others to form complex bodies which eventually dissolve when they experience forms of matter that aid in their dissolution. Thus, over time, plants, metals, animals, and humans grow, expand, and increase in their own system of order as a result of the attraction to matter that helps each grow and strengthen. We seek out forms of matter that are pleasing to us and that strengthen us while trying to avoid those that weaken and destroy our existence. So as not to separate physical and moral laws, we are attracted to each other by their desire for unions that we designate with terms like MARRIAGE, FAMILIES, SOCIETIES, FRIENDSHIPS, AND CONNECTIONS. Virtue strengthens and merges these unions while vice relaxes or totally dissolves them. Beings usually move in a manner that is meant to preserve them and strengthen their bodies. They tend to avoid those things that might be harmful to their existence. As it is with all beings, we are a physical and moral being who seeks to avoid injury and attain that which is pleasing. All beings move toward their own conservation. This kind of movement is referred to as SELF-GRAVITATION or INERT FORCE or SELF-LOVE which is nothing more than our tendency to preserve ourselves. It's what causes us to seek out things that bring us pleasure and happiness. Because we love our own welfare it causes us to gravitate toward things that are favorable to our conservation, and avoid that which disturbs our happiness or threatens our existence. These are sentiments that are common to all humans as long as nothing gets in the way of these primitive tendencies. Causes always produce effects. There are no effects without causes. An impulse is always followed by some motion that makes sense and some change that is somewhat remarkable in the body which receives it. So the motion by which a being acts is a result of some cause which is a function of its manner of being or essential properties. We must conclude that all the phenomena we observe are necessary and that every being in Nature, with its given circumstances and the properties it possesses, cannot act other than it does. Every cause has a necessary effect. Fire necessarily consumes combustible matter that comes within its range. We desire that which really is or appears to be good for our well-being. All beings in Nature act in accordance with their own needs for growth and sustenance. Therefore, everything we see is necessary and cannot be different because of the invariable laws of Nature. As such, there can be no perfectly independent energy or separate causes or detached actions in a system where all beings mutually benefit and rely on the action of others. Two examples of this principle, one from physics and one from morals are:

    A whirlwind of dust which appears to be a confused and frightful storm caused by contrary winds that can roll as high as a mountain is, upon analysis, nothing more than particles of dust and drops of water acting as they must. The different energies acting with the properties of the particles involved shows that after the given causes, each particle acted precisely as it ought to and could not have acted in any other way.

In societies where there is a revolution there is not a single action, a single word, a single thought, a single will, a single passion in the driving forces, be they destroyers or victims, that is not the necessary result of operating causes. Everything that happens is due to the peculiar essence of beings who give impulses and the beings who receive them. These beings create a moral whirlwind that can be traced to the minds and bodies of all involved in the revolution.

There is no cause, no matter how small or remote, that does not sometimes create the greatest and most immediate effects on humans. A storm that begins in the plains of Libya could cause atmospheric changes on another continent which could influence the passions of an individual who may influence many others and might ultimately decide the fate of many nations.

We are beings in Nature who act according to the laws appropriate for us. We get and give impulses from and to the beings that surround us. Our actions are always the result of our own energies and the beings that influence us. This is why there is such a wide range of actions and why we see so many contradictions in thoughts, opinions, wills, and actions. The idea that we act due to motion we've experienced is contested by some. We will shed light on this idea in the context to follow. For now let it suffice to say that everything in Nature is necessary and nothing can act other than it does.

Motion, whether it is received or communicated, establishes a relation between different orders of beings. When these beings are within close proximity of each other, the motion either attracts, bringing them closer together, or it repels and separates them. The first strengthens and preserves them while the latter weakens and destroys them. Once combined, they tend to conserve themselves in that mode of existence by virtue of their *inert force*. However they cannot remain in that state due to constant exposure to other beings who perpetually and successively act on them. Their change of form, their dissolution, is necessary to the preservation of Nature herself. The destruction and reproduction of subordinate beings who must submit to her laws, is what she does without intermission and without interruption. All beings must concur, by their mode of action, to the maintenance of her active existence, so essential to the GREAT WHOLE. Each being is an individual in the great family, performing the unavoidable tasks that have been assigned to it. All bodies act according to the laws that guide their unique makeup, without the ability to change, not even for an instant. This is the central power to which all other energies, powers, and essences submit. The plan of Nature is to maintain the whole by continuously changing the parts. She does so by destroying existing relationships and replacing them with new ones. It is Nature that makes a being expand and change, grow and decline, boost and diminish, add and remove, form and destroy, as is required to maintain the whole. As such, Nature tends to her own conservation.

We have described an irresistible power, a universal necessity, and a general energy that are a consequence of the nature of things which act without intermission obeying constant and immutable laws. These laws are the same for the whole as they are for the individual parts that make her up. Nature is an active living whole to which its parts necessarily concur. Without their knowledge they maintain her activity, life, and existence. Nature acts and exists necessarily, and all that she contains necessarily works to maintain her active existence. *Matter and necessity are the same thing; this necessity is the mother of the world.* In fact we cannot go beyond this saying, MATTER ACTS, BECAUSE IT EXISTS; AND EXISTS, TO ACT. And if one asks how or why matter exists we must answer that we do not know. However, reasoning by comparison of what we do not know vs. what we do know we should conclude that it exists because it contains within itself sufficient reason for existing. If we suppose it was created by a being distinguished from it or less known than itself, (which it may be, for anything we know to the contrary) we must still conclude that this being is necessary, and includes a sufficient reason for its own existence. This admission does not remove any of the difficulty, or shed any light on, or move us a single step closer to understanding the subject. We have done nothing more than create a being about who we are extremely ignorant. We give power to a being that we cannot clearly imagine or demonstrate its existence. Since these beings are created by humans and no two humans are alike, all these beings will be different. As such, all people should be free to believe as they choose. The Hindu has no right to judge the Christian who has no right to judge the Muslim. Each belief system should vow to accept the beliefs of others with respect for the differences. Base your actions on the saying which is consistent with Nature and contains the whole of our happiness – "*Do unto others that which you would have them do unto you.*" Yet it is evident that out of all the variety of systems, according to their doctrines and actions, sadly only one can be right.

In the next chapter we will see how much our imagination has worked to understand the energies of Nature. In so doing we personified these energies and distinguished them from Nature. We'll examine some of the most ridiculous and evil inventions which, in trying to understand Nature, have been imagined. Instead of leading to understanding, these imaginings work to obstruct her course, to suspend her eternal laws, and to place obstacles to the necessity of things.

Chapter 5

Order and Confusion; Intelligence; Chance

In the mind we classified the necessary, regular, and periodic motion observed in the universe as ORDER. This term is a way of thinking about, together and separately, the different relations of a whole which conforms to us. Those things in Nature which we do not understand we classified using the term CONFUSION. It is easy to see that the ideas of order and confusion have no absolute existence in Nature. Everything is necessary and the whole follows constant and invariable laws which require each being, in every moment of its existence, to submit to other laws that come from its mode of existence. As such, it is only in the imagination that we see order and confusion which, like all our abstract supernatural ideas, come only from things we have experienced. The order we imagine is never anything more than humans existing with the beings that surround us, or the whole of which we are a part. So, order in Nature is the observation of a series of actions or motions which we see as moving toward a common end. In a moving body, order is the chain of actions that make the being what it is and allow it to maintain its state. Order, relative to Nature, is the combination of causes and effects that maintain her *active* existence. As has been shown in the previous chapter, every individual being serves to maintain her constantly through the different orders they occupy. We must necessarily conclude that what we call the ORDER OF NATURE is never more than a way of considering the necessity of things which all beings, of which we have any knowledge, experience. Also, CONFUSION is a relative term used to describe a series of necessary actions that result in a change or disruption in a beings mode of existence. When this happens the being instantly changes its mode of action. No one of these actions is capable, not even for an instant, of changing the order of Nature from which all beings derive their existence, their properties, and the motion appropriate to each. Confusion is nothing more than passing from one mode of existence to another, which includes a new series of motions. Order in Nature is a mode of existence, or disposition of particles, that is strictly *necessary*. In any world, including ours, the collection of causes and effects will result in some form of order. Suppose substances that had no attraction whatsoever were combined under extraordinary circumstances.

They would form among themselves a perfect arrangement, a complete order. This is the aptitude within Nature which is to create a being that becomes part of the whole. Order then is the necessity, considered relatively to the connected chain of causes and effects it produces in the universe. The motions within our planetary system are movements that follow necessary laws. The planets that revolve around our sun adhere to these laws as do the moons that revolve around each planet. The earth spins on its own axis as it moves around the sun. As a result we experience SEASONS which result in times of high production and growth and other times of rest and rejuvenation. These effects are the result of gravitation, attraction, centrifugal force, etc. Yet the *order* which we admire as a supernatural effect sometimes changes to what we call *confusion*. This confusion is a necessary part of Nature and her laws. In order to support the whole, some of her parts must be deranged and thrown out of their ordinary course. COMETS with their erratic motion result in feelings of amazement and terror. We experience other forms of *confusion* when the seasons overlap or the weather brings drought or flooding. In times such as these we offer prayers to recall order. What we call CONFUSION is actually Nature following her laws of ORDER which require things to change if she is to maintain her existence. As such, there can never be *confusion in Nature.* Everything in Nature acts as it must.

It follows that there cannot be monsters, prodigies, wonders, or miracles in Nature. MONSTERS are those combinations within Nature that we are not familiar with, yet we must acknowledge as necessary. When we see a mode of action that we are unacquainted with, we use terms like PRODIGY, WONDERS, or SUPERNATURAL to describe those effects. Instead of working to understand the real causes, we rush to an explanation and create imaginary causes. These explanations, like our view of order, exist only in the mind. Our explanations are used to conceal our ignorance and gain the respect of the uninformed by creating causes that are beyond Nature. Because we have not experienced the ideas of which we speak, we prove that they cannot exist. And MIRACLES, which are acts that defy the unalterable laws of Nature, are impossible since nothing can, not even for an instant, suspend the necessary course of a being without bringing the whole of Nature to a halt. There have never been wonders or miracles in Nature except for those who have not studied her laws. It is the height of folly to give supernatural causes to the phenomena we see before becoming fully acquainted with the powers and capabilities that Nature herself contains.

So, *Order* and *Confusion* are relative terms used by people to designate the state of a being. We call it order when the motions of a being lead to its happiness, self-preservation, and are conducive to the maintenance of its actual existence. Confusion is when a being's motions contribute to the destruction of the equilibrium needed to conserve its actual state. None the less, we have shown that this confusion is nothing more than the passing of a being into a new order. When a being experiences rapid change, the confusion intensifies. Death has been a source of great confusion, yet death is nothing more than the passage into a new state of existence. It is the eternal, invariable, and unconquerable law of Nature to which all beings, in their turn, must submit. The human body is no different. It too must submit to the laws of Nature. It is in order when its motions work toward conservation of the whole, which are the preservation of its health and happiness, which is created by promoting the happiness of fellow humans. It is said to be in confusion when it experiences poor health and is no longer working toward its preservation, or certain parts of the body stop performing their specific functions. Sickness produces a new order of motion or a new series of actions within the body. Death, to humans, is the greatest confusion we can experience. In death, the epoch cessation of human existence, the body changes, its parts no longer work, blood no longer flows, feelings no longer exist, ideas vanish, and we stops thinking, feeling, and desiring. The body becomes an inanimate mass no longer able to act in a determined manner. In the new state, which is just as natural as its previous state, the body goes through a process where it dissolves, ferments, and putrefies. Because our essence has changed, our mode of action can no longer be the same. As such, the immutable order of active Nature creates life then dissolves that life to create new life. Every part of this process relative to the greater whole is order within Nature. The stages we pass through in life and in death are our subordinate roles as part of a greater whole. All of our actions are in order whether they are momentary or long lasting. Order in a political society is the effect of a necessary series of wills, ideas, and actions of those who make up that society. The effects work to strengthen the society or they work toward its destruction. We are considered virtuous if we work toward the welfare of our fellow beings. The individual who works toward the misery of others is evil. However, we must realize that both are in compliance with their mode of order no matter how different they are. The relative sense of order within each is complete. It is as necessary for one to promote happiness as it is for the other to induce misery. So, order and confusion in humans is nothing more than naming natural and necessary effects as they relate to us. We fear the evil individual because that person disturbs society and presents obstacles to the happiness of all involved. We avoid a falling stone because it will harm us. Regardless, order and confusion are consequences of the changing or steady state of beings. Just as it is in order that fire burns due to its essence to burn, it is in order that an intelligent and sensible being avoid harm's way, which is anything that can disturb that person's mode of existence.

We call beings *intelligent* if they, like us, can act toward their own preservation and the maintenance of their existence in an order that is convenient to them. They possess the ability to act and move toward a known or desired end result. Beings are considered to lack intelligence when they are not like us, or they do not have the ability to work toward an end of self-preservation. The whole, on the other hand, cannot have a distinct name, or an end, because there is nothing outside of itself to which it can have a tendency. If we create the idea of *order*, we also created the idea of *intelligence*. We will not refer to a being as intelligent if it does not act like us. We will however refer to a supposed being as an intelligent agent or an unseen cause. As such, an intelligent agent acts by *chance* making chance an empty word that makes no sense and is opposed to the idea of intelligence because there is no determined or specific idea that can be associated with it. We attribute to *chance* all the effects we see where the cause is not seen or known. We use the word *chance* when we are ignorant of the causes that cannot be seen yet produce visible effects. When we have no idea how something happens, or when things seem out of order, or when our order is threatened, we call it chance. When we think we see an order of action or a manner of motion we attribute the order to *intelligence*. In reality, because of the way we are affected by an unknown cause, a supposed being becomes the cause and is said to be intelligent. So, an *intelligent being* is one who thinks, wills, and acts toward a specific end. Such a being must have organs comparable to ours. To say that Nature is governed by intelligence is to say that we are governed by a being with organs. Without these organs there can be no sensations, perceptions, ideas, thoughts, will, or an understandable plan of action.

We always make humans the center of the universe, relating all we see to ourselves. When we discover something that is of interest or that pleases, we attribute its cause to something or someone that resembles us. Something that acts the way we act, and thinks the way we think. We form the model for the causes we see from our experiences as human beings. Even though we see a wide range of beings that are very different from us, we imagine a creator within Nature that possesses qualities, ideas, and intelligence similar to our own. We give this being credit for the order we see as well as the things we do not understand. We contemplate to understand the great end of all His actions. As we observed the world around us and all its wonder we realized that we were a small part of a greater whole. We felt it necessary to make a distinction between ourselves and the author of such stupendous effects. Our solution was a cause that possessed better faculties similar to our own. We also gave this being qualities that we wanted and that would make it perfect. As such, JUPITER was given wings and the ability to take any form he deemed convenient. And so, by degrees we formed the idea of an intelligent being that we placed above Nature. We insisted that Nature was nothing more than a heap of dead, inert matter without form and incapable of producing what we refer to as *the order of the Universe*. Finally, some people suggested that the universe was created and governed by an intelligent being. But the more enlightened always responded by accusing them of giving credit for the creation of things that they could not explain to a made up intelligence. Another way of saying this is whenever we saw something in Nature that we did not understand we gave credit to a supreme being that resembled us. In the end, this cause has been personified under such a variety of shapes, sexes and names, that a list of deities, who have supposedly guided nature and been submitted to, makes a large volume of our youthful journey to understand. As we observed confusion and disorder, we were forced to assign these causes new and incompatible qualities. We ignore the fact that disorder and confusion contradicts the plan, the power, the wisdom, and the bounty of this intelligence as well as the miraculous order which He gives it. Unable to resolve the confusion with a benevolent cause, we were forced to create a source for the evil and misery we experienced. Once again we used our own persona as the model for this evil being adding deformities that we had learned to dislike. In multiplying these negative causes we created Pandemonium.

Some will argue that if Nature contains and produces intelligent beings that she must be intelligent or she must be governed by an intelligent cause. We reply that intelligence is seen in beings that come about in a determined manner based on combinations of matter that result in certain modes of action which are given a variety of names according to the effects these beings produce. Wine does not possess the qualities of *wit* and *courage*, yet it occasionally makes people who consume it exhibit those qualities. Similarly, we cannot say Nature is intelligent because of the beings contained within her. She produces intelligent beings by assembling matter that suits their particular organization and whose specific modes of action result in the faculty we call intelligence. These beings, in turn, produce effects that are the necessary consequence of this property. So I repeat, to have intelligence, designs, and views, it's necessary to have ideas. The production of ideas requires organs or senses. Experience proves beyond a doubt that matter, which is regarded as inert and dead, when combined and organized in particular modes, assumes sensible action, intelligence, and life. As such, *order* is never anything more than the necessary or uniform connection of causes with their effects, or the actions a being exhibits while in a given state. *Confusion* is nothing more than a change of that state. So, in the universe all is necessarily in order since everything acts and moves based on the different properties of the beings within it. In Nature there is no confusion or real evil since everything follows the laws of its natural existence. Because all effects are produced with sufficient and substantial cause, the ideas of *chance* and *good fortune* do not exist within the realm of Nature. All causes act according to fixed and certain laws which are dependent on the properties of these causes or beings, as well as the combinations which make up their permanent or changing state. Intelligence is a mode of acting and a method of existence that is natural to some beings. If intelligence is attributed to nature, then we must conclude that it is a necessary faculty used to conserve her active existence. When we stop thinking of Nature as intelligent, or inventing intelligent creators of Nature and her *order*, we will then see that nothing happens by *chance* and there are no blind causes or powers that are indistinguishable from Nature. At this point we can say that everything we see can be attributed to real and known causes, or if an unknown cause it can be studied and discovered. All that exists is a result of the properties of matter which produces order and confusion as it combines, blends, and changes forms. Of the variety of effects that we see, it is we who are blind when we imagine blind causes. We show our ignorance of motion and Nature when we attribute any of its effects to *chance*. We continue in our child-like state when we give credit to an intelligence that resembled us. We created thousands of Gods who control the parts of Nature which we could not. We distinguished them from Nature, gave them properties similar to our own but more powerful, and believed we understood them with obscure ideas which we never dared to define or analyze.

Chapter 6

Moral and Physical Distinctions; Origins

In this chapter we will apply the general laws we have discussed to the beings of Nature that interest us the most. Let's compare humans with other beings on the planet. Let's see how we are the same, how we differ, and if we act according to the laws of Nature. Finally, let's see if our ideas about ourselves and our existence are realistic or fantasy.

We are one of many beings that exist in Nature. We are distinguished from other beings by our actions and our varied forms of movement, some which are simple and can be seen, and some which are complex and not visible to the human eye. Life is nothing more than a succession of necessary and connected motions which bring about perpetual changes to the body caused by blood, nerves, fibers, flesh, and bone. Solid and liquid matters, as well as outside sources like food, air, and anything that makes an impression on the senses, bring about a wide range of changes in the human body. Like all beings in Nature, we constantly deal with destructive forces. At times we seek out such forces and at other times we avoid them. We will now examine these kinds of actions more closely. What we will see is that no matter how marvelous, hidden, secret, or complicated the modes of action that the human body experiences are, they always adhere to the laws of Nature. She brings beings into existence, she sees to their growth and conservation, and she ends by decomposing them, obliging them to change their form.

A human being, in our origin, is an imperceptible point, a speck without form or parts or senses, and as such has no SENTIMENTS, FEELINGS, THOUGHTS, INTELLIGENCE, FORCE, REASON, etc. In the womb, a place suitable for growth, this point unfolds, extends, and increases as a result of the continual addition of matter that aids in our development. We leave the womb, which was so appropriate for our conservation, allowing us to grow, strengthen and develop habits essential for existence, to embark on the stages of infancy. As an adult we have grown and move with purpose. Our actions are visible and we are aware of all our parts. We are a living active mass that feels, thinks, and fulfills functions specific to beings of our species. But how do we become sensible? Because we are always moving toward the maintenance of our own existence, we are attracted to forms of matter that contribute to our individual preservation. We continually combine ourselves with matter that is inert, insensible, and inanimate, to make up a living whole that feels, judges, reasons, wills, deliberates, chooses, and labors fairly efficiently on its own behalf. All the changes we experience over the course of a lifetime, be they external or internal, are either favorable or prejudicial to our existence; either maintain its order or throw it into confusion; are either in conformity with or repugnant to the essential tendency of our specific mode of being. We are compelled by Nature to accept some and to reject others because some make us happy while others make us miserable; some become objects of desire while others we must avoid; some make us feel confident while others leave us trembling in fear. Yet everything that happens to a human being, from the moment we leave the womb to the moment of death, are nothing but a series of necessary causes and effects, which are common to all beings and strictly conform to the laws of Nature. All our modes of action including all sensations, ideas, passions, every act of will, and every impulse that we either give or receive are the necessary consequences of our own specific properties and those that we are exposed to by the beings that move us. Everything we do, be it concealed motion or visible action, are the effects of inert force or self-gravitation which are the attractive or repulsive forces contained within our machine. These are tendencies common to all beings that lead to one's individual preservation. Nature does nothing more than clearly show how we differ from other beings of a different system or order.

When we first contemplated ourselves we mistakenly decided that we move by ourselves and always act by our own natural energy. In other words, in our actions, in the will that gives us impulses, we are independent of the general laws of Nature. Of course the objects which continuously act upon us, frequently without our knowledge and always in spite of us, obey the laws of Nature. If we would take the time to examine ourselves, we would see that none of our motions are spontaneous. Our birth had its own causes, none of which we had any control over. From the moment of birth to the moment of death, we are continually moved by causes which, in spite of ourselves, influence the body, modify existence, and affect our conduct. The slightest reflection would show that the fluids and solids that make up the body, as well as the concealed mechanisms which we believe are independent of exterior causes, are in fact perpetually under the influence of these causes. Without these causes we would not be able to act. We would see that our temperament, which influences our passions, will, and actions, is not determined by us but is given to us in the form of opinions, which we did not choose and had no control over receiving. The state of the blood, nerves, and fibers result in our overall disposition being transitory or durable, which directly influences ideas, thoughts, fears, and actions. Indeed, the state that we finds ourselves in is influenced by the air we breathe, the foods we eat, and the secret combinations that are part of our machine, and either preserve our order or throw it into chaos. If we would study ourselves, everything we'd discover would convince us that we are nothing more than a passive instrument in the hands of necessity.

Everything in Nature is connected and all causes are linked to each other so that the whole forms an immense chain of events where there can be no independent isolated energy or detached power. From this conjecture it follows that Nature, which is always in action, creates the path that each of us must travel. Nature elaborates and combines the elements that make up the body, giving us tendencies and specific modes of action, which aid in our development and growth, and that preserve us for a season during which time we are obliged to fulfill the tasks required of us. Nature also provides objects, events, and adventures that change us in a variety of ways, giving us impulses that are sometimes agreeable and beneficial, while at other times are prejudicial and disagreeable. And Nature, by giving us feelings and sentiments, has endowed us with the ability to choose those objects and methods that are most conducive, suitable, and natural to our conservation. When we have run our course it is Nature who sees to our destruction, dissolving the union of our elementary particles, and requiring us to adhere to the universal law from which nothing is exempt. Motion places us in the womb, brings us from the womb into the world, sustains us for a season, and then destroys us, returning us to the bosom of Nature where we are quickly reproduced and scattered under infinitely many forms with each particle repeating the process of our previous existence.

Human beings, as well as other beings, experience two kinds of motion. The first is that of mass motion which is visible movement of the entire body or a part of the body. The second is internal or concealed motion, some of which we are aware of, while some of it takes place without our knowledge and is only known by the outward effect it produces. In a machine as complex as a human being, formed by so many combinations of matter with such a wide range of properties, proportions, and modes of actions, motion becomes extremely complex. Fast and slow forms of motion frequently go unobserved, even by those in whom they occur. It should come as no surprise that as we tried to understand our existence and explain our actions we encountered many obstacles. We invented some strange hypothesis to explain the hidden causes for motions we observed which we felt made us distinctly different from other beings in Nature. Because we could not always explain our actions, we believed that there was a secret force within us that moved the body by its own natural energy. We believed that we acted according to laws totally distinct from the laws that regulated the motion of other beings. We were aware of some internal motion but how could we know that this internal motion was able to produce amazing effects? How could we know that a fugitive idea, an imperceptible act of thought, could easily lead us into trouble and confusion? We began to feel that within us there was a secret force that was separate from us and that possessed qualities that could control all parts of our being. Without understanding the primitive forces that made a stone fall or an arm move, not to mention the internal impulses that created thought and will, we conjectured that we were not only a distinct being, but that we had different energies than all other being in Nature. From these beliefs we created meaningless notions like SPIRITUALITY, IMMATERIALITY and IMMORTALITY which were used to describe the attributes of these unknown powers which we believed we contained within ourselves. When we could not understand our own actions we contemplated the cause until we personified that cause as a supreme being. We conjectured that it was the only principle of life and activity, and responsible for all forms of motion. We gave it its own form, called it GOD, and worshiped this image of our creation as the source of all good and evil we experienced. To crown this bold conjecture we made this being exempt from the laws of Nature which all beings around us were subject to experience. This being never changed, experienced sickness, and of course never died.

We began to view ourselves as consisting of two different and distinct forms. One is the clump of matter that makes up the BODY. The other we call the SOUL or the SPIRIT. We believe it to be simple, of pure essence, and independent of the body to which it is miraculously connected.

The functions of the body are deemed *physical, corporeal,* and *material.* PHYSICAL BEING is the term related to these traits. The functions of the other we style as *spiritual* and *intellectual.* MORAL BEING is the term designated with the latter. The difference between the two, even though accepted by many philosophers and theologians, is based on faulty logic. We have always addressed our ignorance of things by inventing words, to which we could never attach any true sense or meaning. We imagined that we understood matter with its many properties, resources, and combinations, because we were able to observe it at a very superficial level. However, by associating this matter with substances much less intelligible than itself, we obscured our ability to understand it. So, by creating words and beings, we created bigger problems than the ones we were trying to avoid, while placing obstacles in the path of our knowledge and progress. Whenever we did not have the facts to understand a phenomenon, we resorted to conjecture which quickly became our fancied realities. Our imagination, no longer guided by experience and flooded with new ideas, became lost, without hope of return, in a labyrinth of an ideal intellectual world that we created. It became almost impossible to replace this delusion with truth that only experience could provide. Nature shows us that in ourselves, as well as all objects that act upon us, there is never more than matter acting as a result of its diverse properties and modifications. We are an organized whole composed of a variety of matter, and like all other productions of Nature, follow general and known laws as well as some laws that are specific to us and unknown. So when we ask "What is a Human Being" we answer that we are a material being organized specifically to think and feel. We are capable of change based on the state of the matter that makes up our being. If we ask, "What is the origin of the human species?" we reply that like all other beings, we are a production of Nature who resembles them in some respects and differs from them in others. Most importantly, like all other beings, we submit to the laws of Nature. And if one asks, "Why are we here?" we say the answer is not as important as the fact that we are here. Today, the big bang theory and the theory of evolution are accepted by the scientific community as explanations for how our universe came into existence and how we evolved.

 The process which allows us to live on this planet, also known as relative adaptation, is called the ORDER OF THE UNIVERSE. The want of it is called CONFUSION. Thus, the human species is a production specific to the planet Earth in its current state. If the state of our planet changes the human species will have to adapt, which is to co-order itself with the whole, or disappear. Our ability to co-order ourselves with the whole not only gives us the idea of order but also makes us believe that *"whatever is, is right"* even though everything is what it must be as long as the whole is what it is. So, if we must try to imagine the origin of the human species we might say that we were a necessary consequence of the development of our planet. We came to be as a result of the qualities, energies, and properties that our planet is and has experienced. Our existence co-ordinates with the present position of the earth as well as conditions suitable for human life, and as long as the position and conditions are maintained, we will continue to exist and recreate. When there are changes in either or both that affect our ability to exist, the human species will give way to beings that can co-order themselves with the new or different state of our planet. Indeed humans, like everything else on this planet, are in a state of constant change. It is safe to say that the human species, like all others, vary ceaselessly.

Nature is in a constant state of change, creating and destroying at every moment. To imagine that a human, horse, bird, and fish will cease to exist is difficult for some, yet everything around us is constantly changing. We see it in ourselves and in everything around us. Just as our planet is constantly changing, so do other planets and suns experience constant change. Stars like our sun grow old and explode. Planets perish and disperse themselves to form new planets that may revolve around a newly formed sun or travel aimlessly in space. And humans, an infinitely small part of a planet which is itself an imperceptible point in the immensity of space, vainly believe that the universe was made for them. We foolishly believe that we can control Nature. We flatter ourselves thinking we are eternal and call ourselves KINGS OF THE UNIVERSE!!! Will we ever realize that our time on this planet is short lived? Nature contains no constant forms yet we believe that we are exempt from universal laws and that our species is eternal. In reality we are in a constant state of change. But in our folly we arrogantly assume that we are the KINGS OF NATURE and that the earth and heavens were made for us because we are intelligent. Yet it would only take the displacement of one atom and we would either cease to exist or lose the intelligence of which we are so proud. If you choose to reject the ideas put forth so far and believe that we, the earth and all its inhabitants, the planets and stars, and the entire universe are eternal, we will not argue with you. Whatever you choose to believe will have to be measured by the truths we have learned from experience. We are not meant to know everything, from our origins to the essence of things, but we do have the ability to reason and accept the things we are not capable of understanding, rather than substitute unintelligible words and absurd theories for our uncertainty. To those who believe that the human species descended from a first man and a first woman, it seems clear that we can observe Nature but know very little about the creation of man, *unless you believe the scientific community and the theory of the evolution of man.* The human mind is not capable of comprehending a time when all was nothing, but to use words we cannot understand to explain our origins only acknowledges our ignorance of the powers of Nature and how she could create everything we experience. We have no reason to believe that we are a privileged being in Nature because we are subject to all the ups and downs that her other productions experience. Our pretended superiority is founded in error, arising from mistaken opinions about our existence. If we could look down on the inhabitants of the earth we would see that our species is no different than other creations of Nature. We would see that a tree produces fruit as a result of its energies and its species. Similarly, we act according to our energies to produce the necessary fruits of our actions. We will feel that the illusion which we anticipate in favor of ourselves arises from our BEING which is, at one and the same time, a spectator and a part of the universe. We will recognize that the idea of excellence that we give to our species has no foundation other than to elevate us, and that the doctrines we have proposed with such seeming confidence are based on the very suspicious foundations of IGNORANCE and SELF-LOVE.

Chapter 7

The Soul and The Spiritual System

Humans, after deciding that we are made up of two independent substances that have no common properties, pretend that the impulses that move us interiorly are different than those that move us exteriorly. The first we refer to as a SPIRIT or a SOUL. When asked "What is a spirit?" the reply is that research shows this motive-power, the source of all our actions, to be a substance of unknown nature. It is so simple, so indivisible, so deprived of extent, so invisible, and so impossible to be discovered by the senses, that its parts cannot be separated, even in concept or thought. It begs the question "How can we conceive of a substance which is the negation of everything that we know?" How do we connect ourselves to the idea of a substance void of extent, yet which has the ability to act on our senses, that is to say our organs, which are material and have extent? How can a being without extent move and put matter into action? How can a being without parts influence and move different parts of space? This leads to the important question, "If this substance that is said to be part of a human being is really unknown, undetectable by the senses, and invisible, how did we become acquainted with it?" How did we come up with a substance that, according to all accounts, is not either directly or by comparison recognizable to the mind? If this substance existed and did what they say it does then there would no longer be any mystery in Nature. It would be as easy to imagine a time when all was nothing, when all will be nothing once again, and account for the production of everything we experience, as digging a garden or reading a book. Doubt would vanish from the human species and there would no longer be any difference of opinion since there is only one truth accessible to every seeker.

Natural philosophers and scientist of all time have acknowledged that all things are made up of atoms. Even though they are part of every human being, they are not part of the spirit or the soul according to the metaphysicians. (*Metaphysicians are philosophers who specialize in abstract theory with no basis in reality.*) The philosopher thinks of the atom as a simple being that is homogeneous, pure and without mixture. They admit that atoms have extent and consequently parts which can be separated in thought but not by any physical means. (*Today we see atoms being smashed via colliders.*) Scientific study tells us that atoms are capable of motion, can give and receive impulses which create actions and reactions, are material, are for the most part indestructible, and are in Nature. After studying atoms the scientist forms ideas about them based on research. In doing so, the scientist has formed ideas of them by intelligence and reasoning unlike the meta-physician who puts forth a premise unintelligibly. Wishing to declare us immortal the metaphysicians had to get around the fact that the human body decays when death occurs. To fix this problem we were given a soul which is separate from the body and not subject to the laws of Nature. This spiritual being, whose properties are a negation of all known properties, is consequently inconceivable. If the metaphysicians had knowledge of the atom they could have presented their premise somewhat more intelligibly. Indeed it is the building block of everything including human beings, and it is immortal since atoms are believed to be indestructible elements that exist for all of eternity.

All people agree that motion is the successive change of relations of one body with others or with different parts of space. If a *spirit* can produce or receive motion, that is if it acts on organs of the body, then it follows that it must successively change its relation, tendency, correspondence, and position of its parts with relation to space and the organs to which it gives impulses. It follows that this spirit must have extent and solidity which is to say it must have distinct parts. When a substance possess these qualities it is called MATTER and can no longer be referred to as a simple being as it is described by theologians. It is clear that in order to explain that which they did not understand, the metaphysicians supposed an immaterial substance within us that is not part of the body. They have imagined a negative quality which they can never understand. Only matter can act on our senses and without the impulses provided by matter nothing is capable of making itself known to us. They ignore the fact that a being without extent is neither capable of moving itself or communicating motion to the body since it has no parts, and therefore cannot change its relation or distance relative to other bodies. It cannot excite motion in the human body which is itself material. Suppose the soul moves within our bodies and creates motion, which is a property of matter. If the arm is moved by an impulse from the soul, the force of the movement should be much greater since the mass behind the motion involved is more than the mass that normally moves the arm. The soul shows its materiality when the human body encounters obstacles. The arm may be moved by its impulses when there is nothing opposing it, yet the arm fails to move when it encounters weight beyond its strength. We see a mass of matter that annihilates the impulse given by a spiritual source. You would think that a spiritual source that has no analogy with matter would have no problem moving the world, an atom, or the universe. From this discussion it is fair to conclude that such a substance is a being of the imagination. It is a being that is required to be differently endowed and constituted to set matter into motion and create all that we behold. Regardless, it is a being the metaphysicians have declared as the creator and Author of Nature. As we wondered about this creator and saw ourselves as the model we soon imagined a universal spirit without extent that exists within us. Then we very conveniently gave it credit for all things we did not understand while associating ourselves with the Author of Nature. At this point we felt qualified to explain the connection of the soul with the body. Our self-complacency prevented us from seeing that we were enlarging the circle of our errors by pretending to understand things that we will probably never know. Our self-love prevented us from feeling that whenever we punished someone for not thinking as we did, we committed the greatest injustice, unless we could prove beyond a doubt that we were right and the other wrong. We could not see that since our doctrine was founded on hypothesis and imagination that it might be wrong? Instead GALLILEO was persecuted because the metaphysicians and theologians of his day chose to make others believe what they clearly did not understand themselves.

The moment I feel an impulse or experience motion, I must acknowledge extent, solidity, density, and impenetrability in the substance that I receive the impulse from, or that I see move. So when action is attributed to any cause I'm obliged to consider it MATERIAL. I may not know its individual nature or its mode of action or its generic properties but I cannot deceive myself regarding general properties that are common to all matter. My ignorance is only increased when I imagine a being that does not have the faculties to move itself or give impulses or act. As such, the term, 'a spiritual substance' that moves itself and gives motion to matter and acts, implies a contradiction that necessarily infers a total impossibility. Those who support the idea of spirituality believe they answer the problems they've created by asserting that *"the soul is entire – is whole under each point of its extent."* If an absurd answer will solve problems, they certainly have done it. But if we examine this reply we can see that this invisible part, the soul, no matter how small or undetectable, is something. If this substance, which has no dimensions, were repeated infinitely many times it would be a substance with extent. This can't be what they mean because this would make the soul as infinite as the Author of Nature whom they claim to be a being that is an infinity of times whole in each part of the universe. No matter how much solidity the soul has, when the body moves forward the soul is not left behind, it moves with it. This means the soul has the qualities of matter that are found in the body. So, what conclusion must we derive about the immaterial soul that is dependent upon the body for movement? Without the body is the soul dead and inert, or is it part of a two-fold machine moved forward by its connection with the whole? If so, it resembles a child's puppet, which the child moves for its pleasure by manipulating strings. Because we have not been able to learn from our experiences and use our ability to reason, we formulated incorrect ideas about the concealed principle of motion. If we could let go of our prejudice and gratuitous beliefs we would set aside the error of our ways. We would think of the soul as part of the body that goes through all the stages that the body experiences. The soul experiences birth and death, growth and maturation, happiness and sorrow, health and sickness, and it cease to exist when the body expires.

In our desire to connect the soul with the body while differentiating the two, we made the soul inconceivable but still able to exist in the body and affect the body's manner of acting. The word *spirit* brings to mind the wind or breathing. To say *the soul is a spirit* means its mode of action is like breathing, which though invisible produces very visible effects. Of course breath is material and not a simple or pure substance which is the designation given to SPIRIT. How interesting that in Hebrew, Greek, and Latin the synonym for spirit is *breath*. Only the metaphysicians can say why they chose a word that is used to label a substance they have distinguished from matter. Some, who feared that they were not distinct beings, went further describing humans as beings made of three substances, BODY, SOUL, and INTELLECT. The word *spirit* is quite old and its meaning has changed over the years. The idea of the spirit as it is thought of today is a product of the imagination. PLATO and PYTHAGORAS, no matter how brilliant and imaginative they were, understood spirit as an immaterial substance without extent and devoid of parts. This view is similar to the way we think of the soul but in our view it's the hidden author of motion. The ancients, when defining the word spirit, wanted to describe a matter of extreme subtlety and purer quality than that which acts grossly on our senses. As such some have regarded the soul as a ghostly substance while others as igneous (extremely complex) matter and still others have compared it to light. Over time the soul was given qualities like motion, harmony, and was even said to enable motion in living bodies. For the most part it was thought of as a material substance. Eventually the human soul and the soul of the world became *pure spirits,* or immaterial substances, which are impossible to form any accurate idea about. By degrees, this incomprehensible doctrine of spirituality, which is undoubtedly consistent with the views of those who wish to annihilate reason, prevailed over others. Is it fair to ask that if these false doctrines were created by humans, who are known to error quite frequently, who is most responsible? A thorough investigation shows that the reasoning and evidence to support this dogma were based on enthusiasm and error. Before DECARTES, to whom the world owes the Newtonian System, the soul had been thought of as material. When he declared that, *"that which thinks ought to be distinguished from matter,"* he rather hastily declared that the soul, that which thinks in humans, is a spirit or a simple indivisible substance. Perhaps it would have been more logical and consistent with reason to say that humans, who are matter and know nothing but matter, can think and therefore matter can think. In other words, in particular modifications matter is capable of thought. Regardless, this doctrine was believed to be divine and supernatural because it was inconceivable to people. Anyone who believed the prior belief, *that the soul was material,* were thought of as madmen or treated as enemies to the welfare and happiness of the human race. Once we renounced experience and cast aside reason, we consistently sunk to new levels of confusion fueled by the ravings of the imagination. We satisfied ourselves by constantly sinking to the most profound depths of error. We congratulated ourselves on our discoveries, our pretend knowledge, while all the time our understanding became cloaked in a mist of darkness and surrounded with clouds of ignorance. So, reasoning with false principles and giving up on the evidence provided by our senses, we transformed the concealed author of motion into a mere being of the imagination. It is something that we cannot comprehend because we stripped it of all known properties and gave it properties that make it impossible to understand.

    The doctrine of spirituality as it now exists offers nothing but vague ideas or no ideas at all. It presents to our minds a substance with properties that our senses cannot detect. Can it be true that we have within us a being without extent or parts, yet it can still interact with matter without any point of contact? Also, can it receive impulses of matter through material organs? Is it possible to conceive the union of the soul and the body and comprehend how a material body can hold within it a fugitive being that escapes all our senses? Is it honest to answer these questions by saying they are the product of a mystery, the effects of a power that is more inconceivable than the human soul, and is also concealed from our view? Do we show our ignorance when we look to solve problems through miracles or divine intervention? And to compound our ignorance we are told to believe that the soul, this immaterial substance, can and will be burnt as punishment with fire in purgatory or hell. Don't we have a right to believe that anyone who tells us this is trying to deceive us or that they do not understand the concepts they so anxiously want us to accept as truth? Some of the greatest minds have tried to explain the spirituality of the soul, an intangible substance, with the physical actions of a material being. We should not be surprised by these subtle theories, which are as ingenious as they are unsatisfactory. They try to explain how the soul reacts with beings and its union with the body. When the human mind allows itself to be guided by enthusiasm, authority without proof, and it rejects the evidence of its senses, it can only sink deeper and deeper into error.

If we want to have clear and easily understood ideas about the soul, we must resort back to our experiences, let go of prejudices, and avoid theological conjecture. We must tear away the bandages that we were told are necessary, but were actually used to blindfold us and confuse our ability to reason. If we wish to move to a state of virtue we must ask the natural philosopher, the anatomist, and the physician to combine their experiences and compare their observations about a substance that is so disguised and hidden by absurdities that it cannot easily be known. Perhaps their findings will guide these important functions of societies: **moralist,** the true motivational powers that should influence our actions; **legislators,** the true motives that should excite us to work toward the welfare of society; **rulers,** the means of making their subjects truly happy and giving a united sense of power to all. Physical souls have wants and demand physical happiness. These are real needs and desires and preferable to the fanciful imaginings that the minds of people have been misled with for so many centuries. Let's work to perfect our morality, make it agreeable and excite a passionate thirst for purity. When we do this we will see improvement in our morals and our happiness. The soul will be more calm and serene and we will be moved to a life of virtue because of the motives presented to us. The diligence and care that legislators use to encourage the understanding and acceptance of a natural philosophy will result in citizens whose lives are robust, healthy, and happy, all necessary for the soul. When the body is suffering and nations are unhappy, the soul cannot be in a proper state.

"*mens sana in corpore sano,* a sound mind in a sound body will always make a good citizen"

The more we reflect the more we will be convinced that the soul, instead of being distinguished from the body, is the body itself, which performs all the functions of life and modes of existing while enjoying life. The soul is relative to our ability to think, feel, and act in a mode specific to our nature. Think of our nature as properties, particular organization, and modifications, be they temporary or lasting, that we experience over the course of a lifetime. Those who distinguish the soul from the body have only distinguished their brains from themselves. Indeed, the brain is the common center where all the nerves from every part of the body meet. The brain is responsible for all operations attributed to the soul. Impulses, or motion, are communicated to the nerves which modify the brain which responds or re-acts with the bodily organ. It acts upon itself and becomes capable of producing within itself a great variety of motions which have been designated as *intellectual faculties*. As a result of this interaction some philosophers wanted to make the brain a spiritual substance. It is only in ignorance that such ideas were suggested, lacking both natural and rational thought. Because we had not studied ourselves we were able to suppose that we had within us an agent essentially different from the body. If we were capable of looking at ourselves we would find it quite useless to explain what we see by imagining and guessing about it. This would only take us further from the truth and the answers we are looking for. The problem humans encounter is that we cannot see ourselves. We cannot at the same moment be within and without ourselves, which we would need to be able to truly study ourselves. We are like a musical instrument that asks where the sound it creates comes from. It cannot see how the air moves as a result of the vibrations created by its movement.

The more experienced we become, the more we will be convinced that the word *spirit*, as it is used today, makes no sense that is perceptible, either to us or to those who invented it, and consequently is useless when discussing physics or morals. It refers to nothing more than an *occult* power used to explain *occult* qualities and actions, and in reality it explains nothing. Savage societies created spirits to account for things that appeared to be marvelous and for which their ignorance did not allow them to see the causes. How are we different from savages when we attribute the phenomenon's of Nature and the human body to spirits? We created spirits within Nature every time we could not identify the causes for the effects that astonished us. Not knowing the powers of Nature, we decided she was animated by *a great spirit*. Not understanding the energy of the human body we conjectured, in a like manner, that it was animated by *a minor spirit*. As such, whenever we experienced a phenomenon that we could not explain we fell back on the idea of a spirit. S*pirit* was the term we used to answer our doubts and rationalize our ignorance. It was this kind of thinking that caused the American Indians to attribute the terrible effects of gunpowder to wrathful spirits sent by their enraged divinities. It was these principles that caused our ancient ancestors to believe in a plurality of Gods, ghosts, and many other spiritual beings. Following the same kind of thinking, should we give spirits credit for forces like gravity, electricity, magnetism, etc.? How interesting that priests from all periods of time strenuously upheld belief systems which were consistently proven wrong. In their time they were the craftiest or the most ignorant of people. Where are the priests of Apollo, of Juno, of the Sun, and a thousand others? Yet these are the people who, through the ages, persecuted those who were the first to give natural explanations for the phenomena of Nature, men like ARISTOTLE, GALLILEO, etc.

Chapter 8

Intellectual Faculties Derived From The Faculty of Feeling

In order to prove that the abilities we refer to as *intellectual* are nothing more than certain modes of existence, or a limited way of acting, which result from the specific organization of the body, all we have to do is analyze them. Feelings are nothing more than the brain sending and receiving impulses. We know that it is entirely the brain that is responsible for feelings, intelligence, and intelligence differences, not only between humans and beast but between the person of wit and the fool; between the thinking individual and the ignorant; between the person of sound understanding and the madman. Experience tells us that people who use their intellectual faculties have more functional brains then others. We know that the sensibility of the brain and all its part is a fact. If one were to ask "When did the brain acquire this property?" Our answer is it's a result of the arrangement of, or a combination specific to, the animal. So when a human, who is a sensible being, consumes bread, milk, wine, and other forms of nourishment they become part of the whole and insensible matter becomes sensible in combining itself with a sensible whole. Some philosophers think that all matter is sensible, in which case it would be useless try to explain how it became sensible. If we accept this premise, then just as there are two kinds of motion in Nature, one called *live* force and one called *dead* or *inert* force, then two kinds of sensibilities can be classified, one as active or alive and the other as dead or inert. Then to animalize a substance is to allow it to become active or sensible. So, in fact, sensibility is either a quality that is communicated by motion and which is acquired by arrangement or it is inherent in all matter. In both or either case the human soul, which does not have extent or parts, cannot be the cause of, or submitted to, the property of sensibility. We can also conclude that all parts of Nature have the ability to become animated. The state in which the animation occurs can vary greatly. Life is the perfection of Nature and all her parts contribute to it in different ways. Life in an insect, a dog, or a human is differentiated only by the combination and structure of the organs. If we ask "What is necessary to animate a body?" we reply that it needs no outside aid and the power of Nature combined with its organization are all that is required.

The bodies of animals and humans are designed for movement, both as a whole and the individual parts, and both internally and externally. The nerves and fibers that spread throughout the body and converge at the brain, which is quickly informed of any sensations at even the most remote appendages, is easily modified due to its delicate nature. Air, electricity, and water, all which move very quickly and are in the make-up of the fibers found in the body, contribute to the quickness with which information moves from the extremities to the brain. In spite of the interior and exterior mobility that we are capable of, we are not always aware of the impulses we receive until they shock the brain. For example, we do not feel the action of air until it penetrates the skin at which time the brain is warned of its presence. When in a deep sleep we cease to feel. Outside of the continuous motions we feel, we do not appear to feel motions to which we have grown accustom. In a state of health the brain does not receive distressing impulses, but when in a state of grief or sickness nerves are contracted, shocked and agitated with violent and disorderly motion. These impulses inform us that something is disrupting the natural condition of the affected organ. At other times considerable changes occur that we are not immediately aware of at the time they happen. In the heat of battle a soldier may not realize that a wound has been inflicted because of all the motions being experienced. When many causes are acting on us all at once in rapid succession, we do not notice them; we lose our senses and are deprived of feeling. So, we experience feeling when the brain clearly identifies impressions made on organs with which it has contact. The distinct shock and modifications that we experience are referred as *conscience*. Conscience is the act of reflecting, by means of which I know that I think, and that my thoughts, or my actions belong to me, and not to another. From this it appears that feeling is a mode of being and a marked change produced on our brain. This change is sometimes caused by impulses communicated to our organs either by interior or exterior agents in a lasting or temporary manner. Our organs can be stimulated by interior impulses that make us aware of internal changes that are taking place. The brain is modified and it controls the modifications to the organ. We should not be surprised that the brain is warned when something as complicated as the human body experiences shocks, impediments, and changes. All parts of the body are connected to the brain and are, by their essence, in a continual state of action and re-action.

When a person experiences gout the pain is obvious. The marked pain it produces is felt interiorly without realizing that it is completely due to exterior causes. Diet, temperament, heredity, and many other causes combine, by degrees, to create the acute pain that is experienced. The brain remembers the pain to the point that even when the pain is gone it can be interiorly excited to recreate the pain. Without ever feeling it we cannot form any idea of its excruciating torments.

When visible organs of a body send impulses to the brain they are referred to as *senses*. The various modifications the brain receives are referred to as *sensations, perceptions* and *ideas*. These terms designate nothing more than the changes produced in the interior organ as a result of impressions made on exterior organs when outside bodies come into contact with them. These changes are referred to as *sensations*. When the brain is warned of their presence they become *perceptions*. They become *ideas* when the brain is able to identify the cause that produced the change. So, every *sensation* is nothing more than the shock given to an organ, every *perception* is the shock being sent to the brain, and every *idea* is the image of the object that caused the sensation and perception. From this we can clearly see that if the senses are not moved there can be no sensations, perceptions, or ideas. How can anyone doubt such an evident and striking truth?

We are distinguished from beings that are insensible or inanimate by our extreme mobility. The degree of mobility that each individual possess is what differentiates us from each other and is responsible for the infinity of differences found in the physical and intellectual faculties. From this mobility, which is more or less remarkable in each human being, comes wit, sensibility, imagination, taste, etc. For now we will focus on the operation of senses and the ways they are acted on and changed by exterior objects. Then we will examine the re-action of the brain.

The delicate and movable eyes give us the sensations of light and color which gives the brain a distinct perception by which we form an idea based on the action of the radiant and colored bodies. As soon as the eyelids are opened, the fluids, fibers, and nerves that make up the retina are excited by shocks which they communicate to the brain. Images are defined and color is determined as well as the size, form, and distance of these bodies. This is how we define the mechanism of *sight*.

The fibers and nerves that form the texture of the mobile and elastic skin that covers the human body account for the impulses sent to the brain when the human body comes into contact with another body. The brain notices the presence, extent, roughness, smoothness, pressure, size, etc. of the outside body. The brain forms distinct perceptions which lead to ideas about the object. This is how we describe *touch* or *feeling*.

The delicate membranes that cover the inside of the nose are easily irritated by the invisible and vague odors that come from scented bodies. Due to this activity sensations are excited, the brain has perceptions and forms ideas. This is how we define the sense of *smelling*.

The mouth, which is filled with movable senses, nerves, and irritable glands, becomes saturated with juices that aid in the breakdown of saline substances and is affected in a very lively manner by the elements which pass through it for the nourishment of the body. These glands transmit impressions to the brain which lead to perceptions and consequently ideas follow. It is this process that results in *taste*.

The ear is designed to receive various impulses of diversely modified air which it communicates to the brain in the form of shocks or sensations. These create perceptions of sound and generate the idea of the bodies creating the sound. This process makes up *hearing*.

These are the only ways that humans receive sensations, perceptions, and ideas. The successive changes to the brain are produced by objects that give impulses to the senses. They become causes which produce changes in the soul which we call *thought, reflection, memory, imagination, judgment, will,* and *action*. However, the basis for all of these are *sensations*.

In order to understand the notion of *thought* we will examine, step by step, what we experience in the presence of any other object. Let's say the object in question is a peach. The first two things we notice via the eyes are the color and that it is round. In other words it produces two modifications which are transmitted to the brain which become two new perceptions, or two new ideas designated by the terms color and roundness. Consequently we have an idea of a body possessing color and roundness. If we touch this fruit the organ of feeling is set into action. The hand experiences the new impressions of *softness, coolness,* and *weight* which result in three new impressions in the brain which result in three new ideas. If we hold the peach close to our nose the organ of *smelling* is activated. New impulses are sent to the brain and new perceptions arise which result in the idea of *odor*. If we take a bite of the fruit the organ of taste becomes affected in a very lively manner. This impulse is sent to the brain and is followed by a perception that generates the idea of *flavor*. In combining the different sensations, perceptions, and ideas that result from the impulses we have received we have an idea of a whole which we call a peach which then becomes part of our thoughts. From this we can see that thought has a beginning, duration, and an end, or a generation, a succession, and dissolution, like all other forms of matter. Like them, thought is excited, determined, increased, divided, compounded, simplified, etc. So, if the soul thinks and is an inseparable part of a human being, how is the soul capable of memory or forgetfulness? What makes it capable of thinking successively, of division, of abstraction, of combining, of extending its ideas, of retaining them, or of losing them? How can it stop thinking? There is no divisibility of form in Nature. Therefore it must be concluded that the forms of matter and the thoughts that result are indivisible as well. This discussion sufficiently shows the generation of sensations, perceptions, and ideas and their connection in the brain. It will be seen that these changes come from nothing more than a series of impulses which exterior organs transmit to the brain. It enjoys the faculty of thought, which is the ability to feel in itself the different modifications it has received, or perceive the various ideas which it has generated. Indeed, it can take ideas and combine them, separate them, extend them, edit them, compare them, renew them, etc. As such we will show that thought is nothing more than the perception of certain modifications, which the brain either gives to itself, or has received from exterior objects.

The brain not only perceives the outside signals it receives, but it has the ability to modify itself. When considering the changes that take place in the brain, one interesting operation is its ability to form new perceptions and new ideas. The exercise of this power, to fall back on itself, is called *reflection*. From this it appears that for humans to think and reflect is to feel or perceive the impressions, sensations, and ideas which have been sent to the brain by objects which send impulses to the senses, and consequently produce various changes within the brain.

Memory is the brains ability to renew within itself modifications it has received. In other words, it can put itself in a state similar to one created by specific sensations, perceptions, and ideas that were produced by exterior objects. It does so in the exact order it received them, without any new action on the part of these objects, or when the objects are absent. The brain identifies that these changes conform to those that it formerly experienced in the presence of the objects to which it relates or attributes them. Memory is faithful when these changes are exactly the same. It is treacherous when they differ from those which the organs have experienced exteriorly.

Imagination is the only faculty of the brain whereby it forms new perceptions, or modifies itself, based on impulses it has previously received through the actions of exterior objects on the senses. The brain then takes ideas it recalls and combines them to form a whole, or a collection of modifications which exist only within it. Of course, parts of the individual ideas, or parts of the ideal whole, have been communicated to the brain by impulses the senses have received from exterior objects. This process is how we form the idea of a *centaur*, a being composed of half man and half horse, or a *hippogriff*, a horse with wings composed of a horse and a bird of prey, and thousands of other objects that are equally ridiculous. The brain uses memory to renew sensations, perception, and ideas that it has received or generated, and recalls objects that have actually moved its organs. Imagination combines these objects inconsistently, and forms new objects that have not moved its organs to replace them. So, by combining many ideas we have taken values and characteristics important to us like justice, wisdom, goodness, intelligence, etc. and with the aid of imagination, have formed a variety of ideal beings, or imaginary wholes, like the Greek gods and the modern versions of God and Satan.

Judgment is the ability of the brain to compare modifications it receives, or ideas it creates, with each other in an attempt to discover their relations, or their effects.

Will is the ability of the brain to send impulses to the organs of the body that put them into action. The kinds of actions produced aid to modify the organ to strengthen it, or to keep it from injury. To *will* is to be moved to *action*. The exterior objects, or interior ideas, that result in this disposition are called *motives*, because they inspire action, or cause the organs of the body to move. When the eyes see fruit hanging on a tree the brain is modified so the arm reaches to take the fruit. At this point the brain is modified again and the hand is stimulated to bring the fruit to the mouth.

All the changes which the brain receives, all the sensations, perceptions, and ideas that are the result of impulses given to the senses, or which it renews within itself, are either favorable or harmful to our momentary or habitual mode of existence. They move the brain to action which is different for each individual depending on their respective temperaments. The term PASSIONS, which are more or less violent, describe these motions of the will that are created by the action of objects on the senses. Passions are the result of the union, or the lack of union, between these objects and an individual's force of temperament and makeup. From this we can say that passions are modifications of the brain that either attract or repel the objects that surround us. As such our actions are subject to the physical laws of attraction and repulsion.

The ability of the brain to perceive or to be modified by exterior objects, as well as itself, is sometimes referred to as *understanding*. The grouping of the various faculties that the brain has access to is called *intelligence*. When the brain is used in a determined manner to exercise the faculties it has access to it is said to *reason*. The different dispositions of the brain, some more constant than others, which cause beings of the human species to act in a certain way are called *wit, wisdom, goodness, prudence, virtue, etc.*

All the intellectual faculties, or modes of action attributed to the soul, can be reduced to the modification, qualities, modes of existence, and changes produced by the motion of the brain, which is clearly, in humans, the seat of feeling and the principle of all our actions. These modifications can be attributed to the objects that strike our senses and the impressions transmitted to the brain. In other words, modifications in the brain are the result of ideas that have been generated by perceptions which were caused by objects acting on the senses, and which the brain can re-produce. This brain, in turn, moves itself, re-acts upon itself, and creates motion within the organs, which are nothing more than an extension of its substance. So the concealed motion of the interior organ makes itself sensible by outward and visible signs. When the brain experiences a modification called FEAR it causes the skin to become pale and the limbs to tremble. The brain affected by the sensation of GRIEF causes tears to flow from the eyes, without stimulation from an exterior object. An idea it re-creates with great strength will have a visible effect on the body, even though there is very little modification which takes place in the brain.

In all this there is nothing more than the brain controlling the different parts of the body. If one wants to argue that the brain does not sufficiently explain the principles of motion or the faculties of the soul, we reply that it's no different than all other bodies in Nature in which the simplest motion, the most ordinary phenomena, and the most common modes of action are inexplicable mysteries that we will never fully understand. We flatter ourselves to think we will ever understand the mechanisms that produce attraction in some substances and repulsion in others, or the communication of motion from one body to another. Yet we are asked to accept explanations about how the soul functions because it's a *spiritual being*, a substance we have not and cannot form one idea about. Let's be content to know that the soul moves itself and modifies itself because it is part of matter which gives it activity. The conclusion we must draw based on the operations and faculties of the soul is that it is *material*.

Chapter 9

Diversity of The Intellectual Faculties; Physical Causes and Moral Qualities; The Natural Principles of Society; Morals; Politics

Nature must diversify all her works. Matter in its most basic form will create many different beings with a wide range of combinations, properties, modes of action, and manners of existing. There is not, and there cannot be, two beings that are exactly alike. When a being is created, the place, circumstances, relations, proportions, and modifications can never be exactly the same, therefore the beings that result can never be a perfect resemblance of each other. Even when we believe two beings to be exactly alike, there will always be differences in the ways they act. As a result of this principle, which like all we've discussed prove to be true, we can see that no two beings of the human species have precisely the same traits, or think exactly the same way, or view things identically, or have the exact same ideas, or act in the same manner. And, even though the internal and external organs of humans appear to look and act the same way when viewed as a whole, the differences are infinite when examined in detail. The human soul, when viewed as a material human being, can be compared to an instrument which is capable of producing different notes. When struck with the same force, each chord produces a different sound that is dependent on a wide range of variables. The body and soul combine to produce the diversified spectacle, the mixed scene, which the moral world puts before us. It is from this that we see the striking differences found in the minds, faculties, passions, energies, taste, imagination, ideas, and opinions of humans. These variances are as great as our physical powers, and like them, they depend on our temperament, which is equally as diverse. These differences give way to a continual series of actions and reactions, which make up the life of the moral world. It results in the harmony that maintains and preserves the human race. This diversity also causes inequality between people, which many societies support in different ways. Indeed, if all people were equal in physical and mental powers, subjugating a person or a group of people would be impossible. The fact that it is possible is what makes morals necessary. Without morals we would have to live in isolation, living and working alone, providing for our own security, and ensuring our own conservation. We are much better off living in a society where we can associate with others, make substantial and intellectual contributions, and feel secure in our existence. In a diverse society the weaker must seek the protection of the stronger. It is important that the weak look for opportunities to improve their situation. In this way everyone can be of service to the society in which they live. Societies frequently recognize and compensate those whose virtues, which consist of good deeds, understanding, and assistance, have resulted in real or supposed advantages, pleasures, and agreeable sensations of any sort. This is how the genius is recognized over the ordinary individual. Thus, the diversity and inequality of the minds and bodies of people make us social beings that are, incontestably, in need of morals.

As a result of the diversity of faculties within the human species, individuals are divided into different classes, each in proportion to the effects produced, or the different qualities that result. All the differences in people come from the individual properties of the soul, or from the way the brain developed. As such, characteristics like wit, imagination, sensibility, talents, etc. are seen differently in people in infinitely many ways. So, some are called good, others evil; some deemed virtuous, others vicious; some are ranked as learned, others ignorant; some are considered reasonable, others unreasonable; etc.

The properties and powers of the soul are the same as those of the body. They always depend on the organization of the body and the permanent or temporary changes it experiences. In a word, they depend on its temperament. *Temperament* is, in each individual, the state of balance that exists within the human body. It varies because the makeup of each individual varies in so many different ways. So, in one we see enthusiasm, while in someone else we see bitterness, and in a third calmness, and so on. Temperament is the result of everything one experiences from the moment each of us comes into existence. In the mother's womb we attract matter that will influence intellect, energies, passions, and conduct. Things like food, air, the climate, education, ideas presented to us, and the opinions we form, all modify our temperament. Since these conditions can never be exactly the same for any two individuals, it is not surprising that there is such variety within the human species. It is no surprise that there are as many different temperaments as there are individuals. So, although all we all appear to look the same, we differ in many ways. The internal and external make up of each individual is just the beginning. The person who exercises and eats well has more energy than the person whose diet is poor and who does not partake in physical activity. All of these causes influence the mind, the passion, and the will, or the intellectual faculties of each individual. As such, an optimistic person is usually lively, ingenious, imaginative, passionate, and enterprising, while the apathetic person is dull, inactive, slow in mind and body, unimaginative and lacking in will.

If we were to study our experiences we would find that morals are the key to the human heart and a healthy body frequently leads to a healthy mind. When we imagined the soul to be a spiritual substance we created spiritual remedies to attend to it, which either have no influence over our temperament or do it harm. The doctrine of the spirituality of the soul has made morals an imaginary science that does not provide any true knowledge regarding what actions will lead to our welfare. If we could draw from our experiences, we would see what things aide our temperament and result in the ability to build strong nations. We would then discover what things would be most proper and most conducive to our existence and interests. We could determine what laws are most necessary to assure happiness, what institutions would be most useful, and what regulations would be most beneficial. Morals and politics would be equally able to draw from *materialism*, advantages that the dogma of spirituality can never supply, or even provide an idea. We will always be a mystery to those who obstinately persist in viewing us with eyes taught to believe in spirits. We will always be a mystery to those who insist that our actions are attributed to a spirit which is impossible to form any distinct idea about. When we seriously want to understand ourselves we will thoroughly examine the things we do that make up our temperament. These discoveries will help us understand the nature of our desires, the quality of our passions, and the sources of our inclinations. It will help us predict our conduct on given occasions and it will guide us to institute changes to correct the defects of a vicious organization, whose temperament is as harmful to the individual as it is to the society of which we are a member.

There is no doubt that our temperament is capable of being changed, modified, and corrected by physical causes. We are all capable of forming our own temperament to some degree. Since all individuals are unique, each must find the right balance of diet, combined with physical and intellectual exercises, to attain that natural condition in which the body functions most effectively. A person who is overweight and unhappy can change that condition through diet and exercise, which will most likely improve self-esteem and happiness. A person who moves from Europe to India will, by degrees, become different regarding attitudes, ideas, temperament, and character.

Although there have not been many experiments about what makes up our temperament, there is still enough if we would make use of them, and put the little experience we have to good use. The air we breathe sends *oxygen* to the blood which invigorates the nerves, muscles, and senses throughout the body. It is the substance we breathe that allows for an active and energetic life. Those who process this substance effectively have strong bodies and healthy organs. From this cause, which is entirely material, we see sensibility, wit, imagination, genius, vivacity, etc. which lead to passions, will, and moral actions. It is oxygen, processed differently in each human being that sets us in motion, makes us active, and provides the heat which more or less makes us alive. This active and subtle form of matter is processed throughout the body and must be constantly replenished. It is essential to all parts of the body including the brain. As such it contributes to our intellectual faculties. When it is too abundant in the body it brings on a sense of delirium, when too little it causes dizziness and loss of consciousness. The ability to process oxygen diminishes with old age, and the remaining oxygen in the body dissipates at death. During life it is essential in creating the electricity that sends signals from the senses to the brain and visa versa. The way individuals process oxygen is certainly part of the great diversity found in each human being and the faculties each possesses.

Based on what we've stated it is clear that the intellectual faculties of humans, aka our moral qualities, come about as a result of material causes which have a lasting or temporary influence over each individual. But what determines the organization of each individual? Certainly some of it comes from the parents while other parts come from foods, climate, and air. It is important to recognize that the things that influence our makeup are all material. And the most noticeable of these characters is the physical sensibility that results in our intellectual or moral qualities. To feel is to be aware of changes as they occur. To have sensibility is to feel promptly and in a lively manner the impressions of objects acting on the body. A sensible soul is only the brain receiving an impulse and re-acting promptly by giving an instant impulse to the affected organ. So we are called sensible if we cry when deeply touched by an unhappy event. We identify this as great grief or extreme anguish in a human being. The person who is excited to a degree of pleasure by music is said to have a *sensible* or fine ear. When we are excited in a very lively manner by the beauty of art or any object that strikes the senses, we are said to possess a soul full of sensibility. Other forms of this physical sensibility are *wit*, responding quickly with humor and creativity in different situations; *genius,* the ability to see relationships and make advancements with complex ideas or movements that contribute greatly to our understanding and appreciation of difficult subjects or activities. Wit is like a piercing eye which sees things quickly whereas genius is the eye that comprehends what it sees with a single glance. True wit sees objects as they really are, and false wit connects things that do not apply to what it sees.

Imagination is the ability to quickly combine ideas or images. It is the power we have to easily reproduce a change to the brain, and connect it to the object that caused the change. In its purest form, imagination gives pleasure by embellishing Nature and proving soundness of the mind. On the other hand, when it combines ideas that don't mix, it distorts Nature, creates false ideas, and is proof of a disordered and deranged mind. So, when the imagination is used to create ideal beings that we like, we forgive the illusion because of the pleasure we get from it. The hideous false creatures of superstition are bad because they are nothing more than the products of misguided imaginations, and can only lead to negative feelings and ideas. Misguided imaginations produce fanaticism, superstitious terrors, inconsiderate zeal, frenzy, and the most terrible crimes. A healthy imagination gives way to a strong preference for useful objects, an energetic passion for virtue, an enthusiastic love of country, and the most ardent friendships. The person whose imagination is weak and misguided is unhappy, physically and mentally sick, and lacks the knowledge of what it takes to be a good human being. There must be enthusiasm for excellent virtues as well as for brutal crimes. Enthusiasm is like a state of drunkenness for the soul which produces good results when its effects are beneficial and poor results when its effects cause confusion and disorder.

When the mind is out of order it is incapable of making good judgments. The imagination is poorly used whenever the body and mind are not working properly. In every moment of our existence we are having experiences, given to the brain by the sensations we have, which become ideas that the memory recalls, more or less faithfully. Facts connecting themselves with the ideas they are associated with constitute *experience,* which lays the foundation for *science.* Knowledge is the consciousness that comes from repeated experiences. In other words, it is the precise study of the sensations, ideas, and effects that an object is capable of producing, either in ourselves or in others. All science must have truth as a foundation. Truth is dependent on the constant and faithful relation of our senses. So, *truth* is the just and precise association of our senses, and we cannot be sure of the accuracy or justness of this association without experience. If we do not have repeated experiences how can we compare and confirm results to prove its truth? If our senses are not working properly how can we trust the sensations sent to and stored in the brain? It is only by many diverse and repeated experiences that we can correct the errors of our first conceptions.

We are mistaken when our organs, either due to defects or the lasting and temporary changes they go through, make us incapable of correctly analyzing our experiences. Mistakes occur when an idea is falsely associated with qualities that the object responsible for the idea does not possess. We are mistaken when we feel that beings that exist only in our imagination are real. We are in error when we think our happiness can be threatened by objects that can hurt us either immediately or by unpredictable consequences at a later time. And how can we make predictions about things of which we know nothing? Through experience we can see that like causes produce like effects. Through memory, the recollection of effects, we form judgments about the effects we can expect from specific or similar causes because we have already experienced the action. It seems that *prudence* and *foresight* are qualities that grow out of experience. When a person is burned and realizes that fire causes a painful sensation, the experience will allow one to foresee that it will cause the same sensation again and again. If we realize that certain actions make people hate us, we will know that similar actions will most likely result in people hating us. Our ability to learn from our experiences, so that we can avoid injury and conserve our existence, can be described with one word, *Reason.* Sentiment, imagination, and temperament may be able to lead us astray through the power of deception, but experience and reflection will correct our errors by pointing out mistakes and putting us on the right road. They will show us what can truly bring happiness. From this, it appears that *reason* is our nature, modified by experience, molded by judgment, and regulated by reflection. The ability to reason requires a moderate and sober temperament, a just and sound mind, a well-regulated and orderly imagination, a knowledge of truth that is grounded on tested and repeated experience, and facts, prudence, and foresight. This will prove that although it is commonly repeated that *we are reasonable beings*, in reality there are very few individuals within the human species who can truthfully be said to possess the quality of reason. That is, people who have the combination of dispositions and experience required to be a reasonable person. It is no surprise that the individuals of the human race who can make true connections from their experiences are so few in number. Indeed, we are born into the world with organs capable of receiving impulses, storing ideas and collecting experiences. But, because of imperfections in the mind and body, experiences are false, ideas are confused, images are badly associated, judgment is erroneous, and the brain is saturated with vicious and wicked systems that influence actions and thoughts, constantly hindering our ability to reason.

It has been shown that our senses are the only means we have to determine if our opinions are true or false, and whether our conduct is advantageous or disadvantageous to ourselves and to others. In order for our senses to make faithful relations by impressing true ideas on the brain, they must be healthy. They must be in a state capable of maintaining ones existence, or preservation, which will ensure permanent happiness. It is also required that the brain be healthy so it can operate with precision and perform its functions with energy. Memory should faithfully interpret sensations from the organs and accurately recall former ideas. Only then will we be able to judge and foresee the wanted and unwanted effects that result from actions determined by the will. If our interior or exterior organs are defective, no matter what the cause, we stop functioning properly. When our ideas are either false or suspicious, we make poor judgments and become delusional, as though intoxicated, and unable to grasp the true relation of things. If the memory is not working properly, if it is treacherous, we lose the ability to reflect. Our imagination leads us astray and the mind deceives us, while our senses, over-run and shocked with impressions and impulses, lead us away from prudence, foresight, and the ability to exercise reason. The feeble person, whose organs limit the ability to move, frequently has a limited and unprofitable experience. Like the tortoise and the butterfly, they are incapable of preventing their own destruction. The stupid man, like the drunkard, cannot reach desired goals. But what is the goal? What is the purpose of humans living on this planet? It is self-preservation and to live a happy life. If you believe this, then it is of the utmost importance to understand the true means, which reason points out and prudence teaches us to use, so that we can constantly reach our goals. Our natural faculties, those being our minds, talents, industry, and actions, are our personal passions which give action to the will. Experience and reason show us that the people we associate with are necessary, can contribute to our happiness, and can assist us with their own unique skills. Experience teaches us how to act in order to gain the friendship and support of others. As we observe the actions that attract and repel, that are approved of or condemned, and the judgments that win others over or push them away, we form ideas about virtue and vice, justice and injustice, goodness and wickedness, decency and indecency, and integrity and dishonesty. We learn to form opinions about others based on the sentiments and actions that we experiences via our associations. Because of the diversity of these effects, we find ourselves discriminating between good and evil, and virtue and vice. These distinctions are not dependent on agreements made between people, or the magical will of a supernatural being, but on the solid, invariable, and external relations that exist between beings of the human species, living together in a society. These relations have existed, and will continue to exist, as long as people live in societies.

Virtue is everything that is truly beneficial and constantly useful to people living together in a society. *Vice* is everything that is prejudicial and permanently injurious to others. The greatest virtues procure the greatest happiness and preserve the most order in our societies. The greatest vices disturb our ability to live happily, perpetuate error, and interrupt the necessary order of society. The actions of the *virtuous* tend to the welfare and happiness of our fellow creatures, while those of the *vicious* create misery and unhappiness for all including the perpetrator. Anything that helps us obtain true and permanent happiness is reasonable. Anything that disturbs our happiness or that of beings that contribute to our happiness is foolish and unreasonable. A person who injures others is wicked, while the person who injures ones-self is foolish and does not know reason or truth. Our *duties* are to learn from our experiences using our ability to reason so that we can reach the goals we set. These duties are the necessary consequence of relations existing between mortals who equally desire happiness and who are equally anxious to preserve their existence. To say these duties *compel us* means that without these actions we cannot fulfill the natural purpose of our existence. Our *moral obligation* is to do what we can to make those around us happy and to draw happiness from our associations. Our obligation to ourselves is to do what we must to preserve our existence and to be happy. Morals, like the universe, originated out of necessity, or out of the eternal relation of things.

Happiness is the state of existence that we wish to be in for as long as possible. It's measured by how long it lasts and by its energy. The greatest happiness is that which lasts the longest. Happiness that only lasts for a short period of time is called *pleasure*. The more lively the pleasure, the more elusive it is because our senses are only capable of so much activity. When pleasure exceeds a certain quantity it changes to *anguish*, or a painful experience that we hope will end. This is why pleasure and pain are said to be closely related. Pleasure without moderation usually leads to regret. It begins with boredom and is followed by weariness and ends with disgust. Temporary happiness frequently turns into lasting misfortune. According to these principles it is important to recognize that humans, who are always seeking happiness, must do so with reason, so as to manage and regulate pleasures. We must learn to avoid those pleasures that will lead to regret and pain in order to create permanent happiness. It follows that happiness cannot be the same for all people because of the diversity that makes each individual unique. This is why so many philosophers disagree on what happiness is and how to achieve it. None the less, happiness seems to be a momentary or lasting state that we accept because it is enjoyable. This state is the result of the conformity between an individual and the circumstances that that person has been placed in by Nature. Another way of saying this is; *happiness is the co-ordination of humans with the causes that give them impulse.* We form our ideas about happiness as a result of our temperament, makeup, and habits.

Habit is the way we think and act. Because our interior and exterior organs repeat the same motion over and over again, they can perform these actions quickly and easily. Most of our actions, from occupations, to influences, to studies, to amusements, to manners, to customs, to clothes, and even to health, are the effect of habit. Things like wit, judgment, reason, taste, etc. which come about as a result of the way we think are due to habit as well. We can also say our inclinations which are things like desires, opinions, prejudices, and ideas, be they true or false, are habits we form about our welfare. Our habits are ingrained over time and, whether right or wrong, they make us who we are, frequently preventing us from being truly free. It is habit that connects one to vice or virtue. Experience confirms this through the observations of the acts of a criminal. The first crime is always accompanied by feelings of remorse and guilt. The second time is a little easier and eventually, this person can completely ignore the early feelings. So, one frequently becomes wicked by habit. We are formed by habits so much that they are frequently confused with nature, and result in ideas that we think of as *innate*. Because we are not willing to examine the source of an idea, which is the brain, the idea sticks. Also, we hang on to habits with all our might. The mind experiences a sort of violent revolution and strong distaste when we try to change a habitual idea. The fatal result is that we are led back to the old way of thinking in spite of our ability to reason.

Habit can be explained as a purely mechanical phenomena as well as being physical and moral. Recall that the soul and the body are one and the same, so any changes that happen to the body also happen to the soul. We learn to speak as a result of habit, and at some point learning a new language is very difficult. In the same way, the brain, which is the interior organ, becomes accustom to attaching certain ideas to certain objects. These connections, whether true or false, develop over long periods of time and result in a painful sensation whenever we try to change or adopt a new idea that counters the old one. It's about as hard to make someone change opinions as it is to make that person change languages. This is why we hang on to customs, prejudices, and institutions that reason, common sense, and experience show us are useless and even dangerous. Habits defy the clearest and most obvious demonstrations which are lost in the passions and vices that time has rooted in us. Instead the most ridiculous systems, the most absurd notions, the most extravagant hypotheses, and the strangest customs prevail because we have learned to attach them to ideas of usefulness, common interest, and the welfare of society. This is why we stubbornly hang on to religion, old and unreasonable customs, laws that have little to do with justice, abuses which make us suffer, and prejudices which we admit are absurd yet are unwilling to eliminate. This is why nations avoid new ideas, thinking it would be too hard to address the evil habits that they've come to believe are necessary for their survival, and even feel they would be dangerous to change.

Education is the only art that can be used to develop good habits early in life when the organs are extremely impressionable. It is through education that opinions and ways of living adopted by a society can be taught and become habits. From the first moments of infancy a child begins collecting experiences. Parents or guardians teach us how to apply those experiences and develop our sense of reason. The first impulses they give us will influence our condition, passions, happiness and how we achieve it, as well as virtues and vices. With the help of teachers the child acquires ideas, learns to associate them, learns to think a certain way, and learns to make good or poor judgments. We are shown objects that we are taught to love or hate, to desire or avoid, and to respect or despise. This is how ideas are transmitted from fathers, mothers, nurses, and teachers to children in their early years. At this time the mind is filled by degrees with truths and errors. Conduct develops and we become happy or miserable, virtuous or vicious, and admirable or hateful. We choose a direction based on the passions we have been guided toward and are either contented or discontented about our destiny. We look for happiness based on the things others have taught us to hold in high regard. Over the course of our lives we will work eagerly to satisfy our tastes, inclinations, and spirits, in proportion to the energies they excite in us and our Natural tendencies.

Politics should be the art of regulating the passions of individuals, directing them to the welfare of society, diverting them into the warm current of happiness, and of making sure they flow gently to the benefit of all. Unfortunately, too often it becomes the detestable art of arming the passions of various members of society against each other. Each bent on destroying the other, their existence becomes filled with jealousies and animosities instead of working toward happiness. *Societies* are usually vicious because they are not based on Nature, experience, and general usefulness. Instead societies are run based on the passions, whims, and particular interests of the leaders. Too often it is for the advantage of the few and opposed to the prosperity of the many. To be useful, politics should be

Nature based, that is it should meet the needs of citizens and strive to form a great society. What are societies and their purpose? They are a collection of families and individuals with a wide range of interests working to meet the needs of each other. In doing so families and individuals will be able to obtain advantages they desire from Nature and industry while living in a secure environment. It follows that politics, which is intended to maintain and oversee the interests of a society, should work to create efficiency that helps reach positive goals and remove obstacles that get in the way of the greater good. When we live in a society we make a commitment to engage in providing services without being prejudicial to any of our neighbors. But, due to the nature of humans to passionately look after their own welfare and indulge in their own fleeting whims without regard for others in society, there needs to be a power to remind them about their true obligations to society. This power is the *law*. Its job is, or should be, to enforce the will of society to fix the conduct of its members and direct their actions toward the general good.

As societies grew it became more difficult for all members to assemble and make their voices heard. It became necessary to choose a citizen to make the will of a large number of people known and executed. This is the origin of all *government*, which to be legitimate can only be created by the free consent of a society. The people who do the governing are called sovereigns, chiefs, and legislators, depending on the way the society would like to be governed. Sovereigns are also called monarchs, magistrates, representatives, etc. Being established solely to provide for the welfare of society, governments power is borrowed and can be revoked whenever the people deem it necessary. They can change the form of government and extend or limit the power it gives to its chiefs. By the unchallengeable laws of Nature, the people always have supreme authority over their governments, because the part is always subordinate to the whole. So, the sovereigns are the administrators of society. They interpret its laws and, more or less, have power, but they are neither absolute master nor are they owners of nations. By an expressed or implied *covenant,* they take responsibility for the maintenance and welfare of society, and it is only on these conditions that society agrees to obey them. There is, or should be, reciprocity of interest between the governed and the governors. Whenever this reciprocity is missing a state of confusion exists within the society that borders on destruction. No society ever bestows its governors the power or the right to cause it injury. Such an agreement goes against the laws of Nature because she wills that each society, just as she does with each individual of the human species, tend to its own conservation. As such, no society can consent to its own permanent unhappiness. In order for *laws* to be fair they must be about the general interest of society, or assure the greater number of citizens the advantages of *liberty, property,* and *security.*

Liberty is the ability to work toward happiness without injuring or diminishing the happiness of others. While working toward liberty we must vow not to do anything to prejudice or injure the liberty of our peers. The exercise of liberty that is harmful to society is called *licentiousness.*

Property is the ability to enjoy the fruits of one's labor. It is the benefits that hard work and talent gain for each member of society.

Security is the assurance that each individual can have the protection of the law over property and well-being, as long as we observe the laws and performs our duties with society.

Justice is the assurance that all members of society shall have the advantages and enjoy the rights which belong to them. Without justice, society cannot promise happiness. Justice is also called *equity* because if laws are applied to all members of a society it makes all members of that society equal. Another way to say this is it prevents the more powerful from taking advantage of the less powerful.

Rights for we the people are everything which society permits each individual to do that will help achieve happiness within the framework of reasonable laws. These rights are limited by the singular purpose of all associations. Society has rights over all its members because of the advantages it gives them. The members of a society have the right to demand from society, or its legislators, the advantages they deserve for giving up part of their natural liberty. A society where the elected officials, aided by laws, do not serve its members must lose its right over them. Chiefs who hurt society must lose the right to command. It is not a country if it does not secure the welfare of its people. A society without justice contains only enemies. Oppressed societies consist of only tyrants and slaves. Slaves are incapable of being citizens. Liberty, property, and security make a country a good place to live. It is true love of country that makes a citizen.

Nations become unhappy because they don't know these truths or they choose not to apply them. They become vile heaps of slaves, with no interactions, no good results, and no advantages for any one. Rulers become absolute masters of societies due to the imprudence of some nations, or the craft, cunning, and violence of those in power. Mistakenly thinking the source of their power is from heaven, and they are only accountable to God, they deny that they have any obligation to society. They become Gods on earth and give themselves the right to govern randomly. This is how politics become corrupt mockeries and entire nations, disgraced and shamed, do not dare to resist the will of their chiefs. Laws become nothing more than the whims of the leaders. Welfare is sacrificed for the special interests of the chiefs. The force of society is turned against itself and its members withdraw to gain favor with the oppressors and tyrants. Factions of such societies are seduced by being allowed to injure without being held accountable, and to profit from their actions. As such, liberty, justice, security, and virtue cease to exist in many nations. Politics becomes the art of favoring a certain group of people and giving them the treasures of society. People of these societies get so used to this kind of treatment that it becomes a stupid and mechanical habit which makes them endear their oppressors and love their chains.

When leaders have nothing to fear they become wicked because they have no concern about others in society, and feel they can follow their inclinations without caution or discretion. Fear is the only obstacle society can use to oppose the passions of its leaders. Without it they quickly become corrupt with no concern for the demands of society. To prevent such abuses society must limit the confidence it places in its leaders by limiting the power it gives to them, and give itself the power to control them. It must create checks and cautiously divide the power it gives in order to prevent abuses. The slightest reflection will show that governing is too burdensome for one person or even a small group of leaders because power corrupts and absolute power corrupts absolutely. The experience of time shows that we are always tempted to abuse power. It's like strong liquor which intoxicates the brain and corrupts the heart. Therefore leaders must be subject to laws, not laws subject to the leaders.

Government influences the values of nations as well as the morals. Just as its care produces labor, activity, abundance, health, and justice, its negligence induces joblessness, laziness, discouragement, poverty, impurity, injustice, vice, and crime. It's up to the government to either promote industry, genius, and the arts, or stifle them. Indeed government, the regulator of dignities, riches, rewards, and punishments, wields influence over our ability to attain happiness by its ability to influence our conduct. It modifies us by giving direction to our passions and making us useful in reaching its goals. In a society this is nothing more than influencing the will and actions of each individual through education, government, laws, institutions, and rational or irrational religious opinions. Actions are the habits of people, which are good when they result in the true happiness, and are detestable when they do not result in the happiness of a society. The latter, which creates suffering, prejudice, and disorder, rarely relies on experience and common sense, and usually is sanctioned by laws, customs, religion, public opinion, or example. As crime abounds virtue shrinks and gives way to vice. At every turn, the most deplorable actions are approved of and applauded by some. Assassinations, child labor, robbery, torture, intolerance, austerity, genocide, and many others such acts have been approved of by nations and governments. Above all, *superstition* has resulted in some of the most unreasonable and revolting customs.

Nature influences our passions through its laws of attraction and repulsion. We are attracted to those things which appear useful and repel those which we view as harmful. Government has the power to put our passions to work or to restrain them with favorable or unfavorable consequences. All of our passions are constantly limited by either loving or hating, seeking or avoiding, and desiring or fearing. These passions, which are necessary to our conservation, are different in each individual and displayed with varying degrees of energy based on temperament. Education and habit develop them and government puts them into play, moving them toward objects believed to be of interest to itself and the people. Names given to these passions depend on the goals they elicit. Pleasure, grandeur, or riches which produce excitement, as well as ambition, vanity, and greed are just a few. The government is usually the source of the passions that predominate in most nations. It is the direction of the leaders that makes some nations warlike, some superstitious, some aspiring glory, some greedy, some rational, and some unreasonable. The reigning powers could easily create an enlightened and happy society, spending only a small fraction of what they spend to make them violent, stupid, deceived, and afflicted. The people could be as wise and happy as they are remarkable for being blind, ignorant, and miserable. The attempt to destroy our passions must be abandoned. Instead direct them toward objects that may be useful to us and beneficial to society. Education, government, and laws should be the guides that restrain our passions within bounds determined by reason and experience. Give us ambitious honors, titles, distinctions, and power when we usefully serve our country. Give riches to those who make themselves necessary to the society. Give commendations and eulogies to those who are moved by the love of glory. Allow our passions a free and uninterrupted path as long as their application results in real, substantial, and durable advantages to society. Education must be focused on that which is truly beneficial to the human species and necessary to the maintenance of society. The passions of humans are dangerous when everything about them works to create evil.

Nature does not make us good or bad. She combines our parts making us more or less active, mobile, and energetic. She gives us organs and temperament, which form our passions. Our passions always have our happiness and welfare as their goal. As such, they are legitimate and natural, and can only be called good or bad relative to the influence they have on other beings. Nature gives us legs to carry our weight and move us from one place to another. We can take care of them and use them for good or evil. The arm given to us by Nature serves many purposes and is neither good nor bad. It becomes criminal when we have developed the habit to use it to rob or kill. We are taught from infancy to desire money and society requires us to have it, but we should be taught the importance of getting it without harming others. The heart is like soil that Nature makes which can grow weeds or useful grains, poisons or refreshing fruit, depending on the seeds planted in it. As an infant we learn to like or despise, to seek after or to avoid, and to love or to hate. Our parents and teachers make us virtuous or wicked, wise or unreasonable, studious or immoral, steady or shaking, and firm or vain. They influence us throughout our entire life, teaching us what to desire and avoid, and what to fear or love. We work to obtain the objects of our desires with the energy of our temperaments, which determines the force of our passions. It is education that inspires within us ideas and opinions, whether true or false, that causes us to act in a way that is advantageous or harmful to both ourselves and others. We come into the world with nothing but the need for self-conservation and happiness. The real or imaginary means of achieving both are presented to us via instruction, example, and customs. Our habits allow us to use these means to secure possession of the objects that we believe will enhance our existence. Whenever our education, the examples we learn from, and the means we use are based on reason and experience, it will all combine to make us virtuous. Our habits will strengthen these characteristics and, consequently, we become useful members of society, securing well-being, happiness, and relationships. If, on the other hand, we are taught at an early age that virtue is useless and offensive, and vice is useful and agreeable to our happiness, we will become vicious. Because of our beliefs we will work to injure society by making those around us unhappy. We will be swept up in a tide of negativity and will renounce virtue, which will appear to be a vain idol with no attraction because it goes against everything we had been taught to believe is desirable and will result in our happiness.

For us to become virtuous we must find value in practicing virtue. To reach this end education should teach us reasonable ideas. Public opinion should lean toward virtue as the most desirable good. Acts of virtue should be pointed out as examples of the most worthy esteem. Governments should regularly reward and honor it. Vice should always be despised and crime consistently punished. Is there virtue within our society? Does education teach one how to attain true happiness, that is true notions of virtue and how to be a contributing member of society? Do we observe examples of innocence and manners which cause one to respect decency, to love integrity, to practice honesty, to value good faith, to honor equity, to admire meaningful relationships and to fulfill ones duties? Does religion, which tries to control our actions, make us sociable, comforting, and humane? Do the leaders of our government faithfully honor and compensate those who have served the country? Are those who have pillaged, robbed, and plundered our country and others, dividing and destroying them, being punished? Is justice administered evenly within the country? Do our laws protect the weak, the poor, and the miserable from those with a distinct advantage? How often do we see crimes committed by our leaders and the wealthiest, justified, often applauded, and sometimes crowned with success, while they arrogantly cast away all semblances of virtue? In societies like this virtue exists only in a few citizens who know its value and enjoy it in secret. For the rest it is a disgusting object viewed as an enemy of their happiness and censor of their individual conduct. It is our nature to move toward our welfare, and if we see vice as the means to attain it then we must love vice. When we see uselessness and crime rewarded and honored we will have no motivation to work toward the happiness of our fellow beings or restrain the fury of our passions. When our minds are full of false ideas and dangerous opinions our conduct is affected, making it nothing more than a long chain of errors and a series of mistakes and depraved actions.

We know of cultures that flatten the heads of their children by squeezing them between two boards, preventing them from taking the shape that Nature intended. Institutions created by people do the same thing when they try to counteract Nature by constraining, diverting, and extinguishing natural impulses and replacing them with others that are the source of all our misfortunes. In almost all countries on this planet, we are deprived of truth, fed falsehoods, and amused with marvelous illusions. We are like a child whose appendages are bound, which deprives them free use of their limbs and inhibits their growth and health. Most of our superstitious opinions promise supreme happiness which becomes the object of our passions. Of course the phantoms presented to our imagination cannot be thought of the same way by all who contemplate them, so we find ourselves in a constant state of disagreement regarding these objects. We hate and persecute our neighbors who believe differently than we do, and our neighbors in turn persecute us, all believing that they are doing the right thing. We create the greatest crimes to maintain the opinion that we are acting correctly. It is superstitions that give us foolish and unreasonable passions from infancy, filling us with vanity and enslaving us with fanaticism. The individual with an active imagination is driven to fury; the restless and hyperactive person becomes a madman who is frequently as cruel to himself as he is dangerous to others; and contrarily, the inactive and sickly person becomes miserable and useless to society.

Public opinion constantly puts forth false ideas of honor, and wrong notions of glory. It praises not only foolish actions, but also those which are harmful. Unfortunately, such actions are authorized by example, consecrated by prejudice, and prevented from being viewed with disgust and horror by habit. Indeed, it is habit that allows the mind to become comfortable with the most absurd ideas, the most unreasonable customs, the most evil actions, and with prejudices that are contrary to our interests. Bad habits lead to the detriment of the society in which we live. Yet we see nothing strange, remarkable, despicable, or ridiculous except opinions and ideas that are different than ours. There are countries where the foulest and most diabolical actions pass for very honest and perfectly rational conduct. In some nations they kill the old men; in some the children strangle their fathers. The Phoenicians and Carthaginians slaughtered their children to their Gods. Europeans approved duels and one who refused was dishonored. The Spaniards and Portuguese thought it praiseworthy to burn a person who did not believe in their God.

Authority is supposed to enforce the interests of the people. However, in many cases, in an effort to maintain its power and interests, it is based on prejudices and errors and is sustained by force, which is never rational. Leaders, who have deceptive images of happiness, mistaken notions of power, and false ideas about grandeur and glory, surround themselves with people who support their delusional ideas. These people have formulated outrageous ideas of virtue. By degrees they influence all who surround them forming a chain of corruption. This is the true source of moral evil. It is everything that works to make us vicious and lead us to acts against society, which results in the misery of most of its members. The strongest forms of motivation are used to inspire us with passion for objects that are useless. As we strive to attain these useless objects, the means we must employ to get them makes us dangerous to our fellow citizens. The leaders who should be guiding us, either impostor's or fools, forbid us to listen to reason by making truth appear dangerous and making error seem to be necessary for our welfare, not only in word but in text. Habit requires us to hang on to irrational opinions, hazardous feelings, and blind passions for useless or dangerous objects. This is why, for the most part, we seem to move toward evil, and the passions that are meant by Nature to conserve us, become instruments of our destruction and the curse of society. This is why societies find themselves in a state of continuous war, creating enemies who envy each other and are always seeking more power. The small number of virtuous people in these societies, those with moderate temperament and passions, who do not desire the kinds of power that consumes their counterparts, must be put into positions of leadership.

Our nature, which comes about as a result of each individual's diverse experiences and physical make-up, determines the whole person. The highly spirited individual will have strong passions while the lazy will have unreal and gloomy passions. The happy person will have cheerful passions while the calm will have gentle passions. The person who is referred to as *virtuous* seems to have a balance of all of the above, where no one passion predominates over another. And habit, as we have seen, modifies our nature. It is formed by parents, teachers, and the society in which one lives. They form our temperament making us reasonable or irrational, enlightened or stupid, fanatical or heroic, one who works toward the public good or an unbridled criminal, and a wise virtuous person or one of vice. All forms of the moral person are determined by the diversity of our ideas, which the brain receives via the senses. Our temperament is the product of physical substances, our habits are created by physical modifications, and our opinions, whether good or bad, injurious or beneficial, true or false, form themselves in our minds and are never more than the impulses the brain receives from the senses.

Chapter 10

The Soul

What has been discussed so far is enough to prove that the *soul* is purely material. Proof of this is seen in the way we get ideas, which is by the impressions that material objects make on our senses. Intellectual capabilities necessarily result from this process. There are those who don't believe this and insist on making the soul a substance distinguished from the body. They make it a distinct entity based on the belief that the soul can form its own ideas. In fact they believe that we are born into the world with ideas which they call *innate,* or *universal ideas*. They believed that the soul, existing in a nature where everything is connected, was given special privileges. They propose that it enjoys the ability to move itself without receiving impulses, to create its own ideas, and to think, all without any external stimulus. And without moving its organs it could create an image of what it's thinking about. Due to these gratuitous theories and strange pretensions, which are all that is needed to refute some very intelligent men who were overtaken by superstitious ideas, they suggest that the soul, without proof or any way to act on the senses, is competent to explain to itself the whole universe and all the beings it contains. There are those who assure us that the body would have no sensations, perceptions, or ideas without the assistance of the soul. Our ability to feel, understand, taste, touch, and perceive material objects that are outside of ourselves is credited to the soul. Others have worked very hard to prove that all we see is nothing more than a magical illusion and the universe exists nowhere but in ourselves and the imagination. This makes the existence of all things difficult by creating an explanation that cannot be proven and is meant to deceive in order to justify the existence of the soul. Yet another crazy idea makes God the common bond between the soul and the body maintaining that the soul and the body are one and that all thoughts come from the soul which is controlled by God, making the body unnecessary. If this is true why are there so many false ideas and errors attributed to the human mind? Questions like these are, according to the theologians, displeasing to God. Nevertheless, to justify such monstrous opinions, they assert that ideas are purely the objects of thought. But, recall that in a prior discussion it was shown that ideas come from exterior objects which send impulses to the senses that modify the brain. Each idea is an effect which we relate, correctly or incorrectly, to a cause. If we only get ideas from material substances, how can we possibly suppose that the cause of our ideas is immaterial? To pretend that we can form ideas of the universe without the aid of material objects is like saying a blind person can form a true idea about a picture that has not been described to this individual.

It is easy to see why so many extremely profound and very enlightened men got it wrong when trying to describe the operations of the soul. Influenced by either their own prejudices, or by the fear of going against the opinion of some superior theologian, they became advocates of the principle that the soul is pure spirit and an immaterial substance whose essences is directly different from that of the body and everything we see. They could not see, or ignored, the connection between material objects and the organs and senses that give us ideas. Yet seeing that the soul did have ideas they concluded that it must get them from itself, and not from external beings which they felt had no way of acting on the soul. They imagined that all the changes and actions of the soul came from its own peculiar energy which was given to it by God. So it gets its energy from beings that we know nothing about and cannot observe or experience with our senses.

There are some things that happen that appear to support the opinion that the human soul can produce ideas within itself and without any exterior help. *Dreams* occur in our minds and do not appear to have any external stimulus, yet they can result in ideas that cause the body to act. A minimal amount of reflection shows that the mind is full of ideas, even during sleep. These ideas are the result of exterior objects that modified the brain at an earlier time. The modifications that excite the brain are recalled during sleep, more or less accurately, and with a greater or lesser degree of conformity to the outside experience that triggered the initial idea. Sometimes the causes of the dream are remembered with great accuracy. Other times the dreams come without order and connection to the real objects that cause them. If someone sees a friend in a dream the brain recalls the image of the friend and the image is nothing more than an effect of memory. If, in a dream, someone sees a monster for which there is no model in Nature, the brain is assembling and associating scattered ideas in a ridiculous manner. As such, in dreaming imagination comes into play. Dreams that are exaggerated, quirky, or unconnected are sometimes the result of a disorder within the body. When the brain is disturbed it has confused ideas that want connections. Suppose, in a dream, one sees a Sphinx, a being described by poets that has a head and face of a woman, the body of a dog, wings like a bird, claws of a lion, who asks riddles, and kills those who cannot solve them. This individual has either seen a representation of one when awake, or the disorderly action of the brain causes it to combine ideas, creating a whole that has no model in Nature. Frequently we dream while awake. A disordered imagination creates images that make no sense, yet resemble outside objects that have communicated ideas to the brain. While awake, watchful theologians have created phantoms which they use to terrify people. They have taken the most terrible traits seen in humans and exaggerated and enlarged them to create ideal beings that leave mortals frightened and trembling.

So we see that dreams, rather than proving that the soul acts on its own and has its own ideas, show the soul is entirely passive during sleep and that it is subject to the involuntary confusion produced by physical causes which affect the body and the soul in the same manner. What appears to have led some to believe that the soul has its own ideas is the fact that they regard these ideas as if they were created by a real being, when in fact they are nothing more than changes in the brain of humans produced by unidentified or unknown objects. If you know and understand the objects, then you know the source of the ideas. This is the basis of all their errors. Dreams mean there is some sort of physical confusion in the body that causes the brain to act abnormally. The soul does not act on its own in any moment of our existence. It works in unison with the body and is subject to everything the body experiences.

If a being really existed in Nature that could move itself, that is produce motion independent of all other causes, such a being would be able to stop itself or stop the motion of the universe. But even that would be nothing more than a huge chain of causes, acting and re-acting by necessary and unchangeable laws. Unless the essence of everything were changed and the properties of everything annihilated, the general system of the world is a long series of motions, received and communicated in succession, by beings capable of giving impulses to each other. Each body is moved as a result of a collision with some other body. We believe in the invisible motion of the soul because we do not see the objects that put it into motion or because we want it to have magical powers. The source of our errors are that we view our body as gross and inert, while we view the soul as a sensible machine which is instantly aware of impressions it gives and receives, is aware of its own existence, has memory, and can make associations. In short, we give it the ability to *reason*.

An idea, which is nothing more than a modification of the brain that cannot be seen, is communicated to others when the tongue is stimulated to speak. Words can create ideas, thoughts, and passions in others. The wills of people are influenced to combine their efforts to produce a revolution in a state, or to have influence over the entire globe. As such ALEXANDER decided the fate of Asia and MAHOMET changed the face of the earth. Imperceptible causes produce the most terrible and the most extended effects as a result of a series of necessary motions imprinted on the brain. Because it's so hard to understand the causes that motivate our actions, some attribute the effects they see to the soul. Aided by the powers of imagination and thought, they propose that the soul is able to leave the body, moving with the greatest of ease to distant places on the planet and in the universe. They believe that a being capable of such rapid motion must be different from all others. They convinced themselves that the soul really does travel or spring over immense spaces to meet with various objects, ignoring the fact that it instantly gets all its ideas from the senses. Indeed, the only way that we become aware of objects and get ideas is through our senses. It is only due to the impulses given to the body that the brain is modified, or that the soul thinks, wills, and acts. ARISTOTLE said more than two thousand years ago, *"Nothing enters the mind but through the medium of the senses."* If follows that every impulse must find a sensible object that it can associate an idea with, like a human, a tree, a bird, or pleasure, happiness, vice, virtue, etc. Yet the principle that the soul can create ideas with its own magical powers and without the senses has been put forth by many philosophers. Whenever a word or idea does not connect with a sensible object it has no meaning and makes no sense. It would have been better for us if the idea was banished from the mind and the word struck out of our language. This principle is the opposite of the axiom, *"If the direct be evident, the inverse must be evident as well."* Yet why is it that many great thinkers who recognize the absurdity of a system of unfounded ideas, are not able to see the immediate and necessary consequences? How is it that they do not have the courage to apply such a clear principle to the fanciful beliefs that have vainly occupied the human mind for so long? This principle so clearly counters the teaching of theologians who want us to believe that there are objects we cannot sense, and therefore never have an accurate idea about except for what they tell us. Unfortunately, when a belief is held sacred it prevents even the most intelligent mortals from seeing the simplest application of the most self-evident principles. When religious beliefs are involved the greatest individuals are nothing more than children, who are incapable of accurately assessing their own data. All those who adopted such a system should have concluded that all the images that religions use to mystify and frighten people are nothing but creations of the imagination. Indeed, an immaterial spirit or substance, without extent, without parts, is, in fact, nothing more than an absence of ideas. We should know that the indescribable intelligence which we are told presides at the helm of the world is a being of the imagination. We have been given a variety of spirits with attributes, of which it is impossible for our senses to prove either existence or qualities.

Similarly, the conclusion that we are born with ideas of virtue, also known as *moral instinct*, is based on nothing more than religious speculation and should be rejected. Before we can judge we must feel. Before we can distinguish good from evil we must compare. *Morals* are a science of facts, and to base them on anything other than our senses makes them meaningless and useless. To assert that ideas of virtue are *innate*, or the effects of *instinct*, is to pretend that we know how to read before we have learned the letters of the alphabet. Indeed, how can we know the laws of society before they have been made or enforced? And a close look at the so called innate morals we are said to be born with shows that they have all come to us as a result of our senses. Some have developed in the mind with great difficulty over long periods of time, but they have never been permanent and they continuously change. The morals that we believe are inherent are actually the effect of education, example, and above all, habit, which through repetition teaches the brain to associate ideas in a confused or correct manner with systems that are either rational or absurd. We think of an idea as innate if we cannot recall its origin. At a certain age we believe we have always had the same ideas and outlooks. For example, most people cannot recall the first time they heard the word God and the ideas and thoughts it generated. From that moment we are always searching for a being with whom to connect the idea which we either form to ourselves or which is suggested to us. Upon hearing about God over and over again, even the most intelligent regard this idea as part of their whole or imprinted on their soul at birth, even though it is clearly the result of the influences of parents, teachers, society, and the changes we experiences due to our individual make-up. As such, each individual forms ideas about God, using ourselves as the model and making modification as we see fit.

Our ideas about morals are not inborn. The morals that guide our actions and judgments regarding the actions of others are based on experience. It is only experience that will allow us to determine whether morals are useful or prejudicial, virtuous or vicious, honest or dishonest, and honorable or condemnable. Our moral opinions are the result of many experiences, gathered over time, which we apply when we judge the actions of our peers. When we are able to use experiences to judge quickly and fairly we are said to have *moral instinct*. The idea of *instinct* is nothing more than the body wanting something as a result of some attraction or repulsion. When a baby suckles the nurse's breast, it is an enjoyable experience that nurtures the young body. It becomes a habit as a result of the repeated experience. The idea that parents and their children instinctively love each other is nothing more than the effect of experience, reflection, and habit. Indeed, parents have been known to treat their children like enemies making them victims of irrational whims and unreasonable desires.

From the moment of a person's birth to the moment of death we feel. We have sensations that we either like or dislike. We collect facts and gather experiences that produce ideas in the brain that are either cheerful or gloomy. No one has all this experience presented to the memory at the same time. It is this body of experiences that directs us, without our knowledge, in all our actions. Because we do not see where our actions come from, we designate some actions as *instincts*, and think of them as magic or the work of a supernatural power. Others see it as a world that makes no sense. The psychologist views it as an opportunity to examine a multitude of experiences that lead to a long train of extremely complicated ideas. Even in animals their supposed instincts are nothing more than the habits they have developed to aid in their survival. Animals have shown that they have passions that can be modified. Only a fool would deny that animals feel, choose, deliberate, express love, and show hatred. In many instances their senses are much keener than those of humans. Acknowledging these facts has caused us to wonder if animals have spiritual souls. Theologians deny it because it elevates animals to the same level as humans. Of course denying it exists in animals gives some reason to question its existence in humans, making us no different than animals. DESCARTES fancied he solved this dilemma by saying that beasts are mere machines with no souls. The absurdity of this statement is obvious when one who views Nature without prejudice will readily see that the only difference between humans and beast is the diversity of our organization.

Some people can make judgments about others by looking closely at the face. Such people are said to have instincts, but are in fact people with very acute feelings. It is certain that the soul, which has been made spiritual, makes marked impressions on the exterior of the body. Our passions can be seen in many ways. Most people know when they are in the presence of a caring individual, or one with evil intentions, or one with a serious focus, or a liar, or open and accepting, etc. A keen eye can frequently see the concealed motion of the soul by the visible traces it leaves on the features of the body. The eyes in particular change quickly to expose the passions excited in someone. Calm eyes are seen in a tranquil person while wild eyes indicate a restless mind and so on. The person who can quickly assess the eyes and the facial marks to make judgments about others is not doing anything supernatural or wonderful.

People of the human species who have a quick or acute sense of perception that allows them to assess a situation and make judgments about the future can appear to be miraculous. A good doctor can assess a disease and quickly come up with a prognosis. Indeed, we frequently see people who can analyze several circumstances and make predictions about distant events, yet there is nothing supernatural about this kind of talent. It indicates nothing more than a person with great experience and sensitivity, which allows them to make quick judgments and foresee distant effects. This quality is also seen in animals who foresee much better than we do. Birds have been prophets and guides to nations who pretended to be extremely enlightened. So it is due to the physical and mental make-up that some beings astonish others. To have *instinct* implies the ability to make quick judgments. Our ideas on vice and virtue are not inborn but acquired like all our ideas. Our judgments are based on our experiences, which are either true or false depending on the habits that formed and changed us. A baby is born with no idea of God or virtue. We learn about these ideas from our parents and teachers. We process them based on our natural organization which is our temperament combined with our world view. Nature gives us legs which we learn to use. Our agility depends on their natural organization and the way we exercise them.

A person's sense of *taste*, as it relates to music, art, design, etc. is sometimes thought to be inborn. In reality it is attributable to the awareness of our senses, which is the development of the habits of seeing, comparing, and judging certain objects. So, it is the ability to quickly assess a situation with all its various relations. It is developed by repeatedly seeing, feeling, and experiencing objects until they are known and understood. As such, the power to quickly judge develops, but by no means is one born with such powers. We must have feelings before we can think and have ideas. We must be moved, either agreeably or disagreeably, before we can love, hate, approve, or blame. Yet these truths must be rejected if one believes that a supernatural power gives us ideas and opinions at birth. For the mind to be able to think there has to be an object with qualities that must strike some of the senses. If we do not have knowledge of any of the qualities of an object then that object is null or does not exist for us.

It may be declared that there is universal consent regarding propositions like *the whole is greater than its parts* or mathematical proofs, which appear to justify the notion that some knowledge is inborn and not acquired. But all knowledge, which is the immediate fruit of experience, is acquired. It is required to compare the whole with its parts before one can conclude that the whole is the greater of the two. We are not born knowing that two plus two make four, but we quickly learn this truth. Before forming any judgment it is absolutely necessary to have compared facts. Those who openly support that we are born with ideas or notions have confused our natural disposition with the habits that modify us. They deny that we have the ability to apply our experiences to make judgments. The person who is an excellent judge of paintings certainly has more acute and penetrating vision, but that person's sight would be useless without ample opportunity to exercise her talent. So the question arises, can those skills which are called *natural*, be regarded as innate? A man at the age of twenty is much different than he was at the time of his birth. The physical causes that are continuously changing us make our natural skills different at different times of our lives. Indeed, we think quite differently about things at one time than at another: when young than when old; when hungry than when our appetite is satisfied; in the night than in the day; when irritable than when cheerful. The way we think and act varies from hour to hour, and is influenced by a thousand other circumstances, which keep us in a state of perpetual inconstancy and instability. We always see children who appear to be very smart but end up seeming quite stupid. We see other children who don't seem to be very bright end up astonishing all around them in their later years. There comes a time when the mind takes a leap forward and is able to draw from a multitude of experiences without the individual's knowledge.

So, it cannot be repeated enough that all our ideas, notions, modes of existence, and thoughts are acquired. The mind can only think about things of which it has knowledge and understands, either well or poorly; that is, things which it has previously felt. Ideas which have no model in the real world are called *abstract ideas*, and are creations of the mind and the imagination. Words that designate ideas like *bounty, beauty, order, intelligence, virtue, etc.* make no sense unless one can explain them, either by objects that the senses have experienced, or when we see a way of acting that we associate with that word. The vague idea of *beauty* means nothing until we attach it to an object that has struck the senses in a specific way, and in consequence defines this quality for us. What does the word *intelligence* mean if it is not connected with a certain mode of being and acting? Does the word *order* mean anything if it is not connected with a series of actions that affect one in a certain way? The word *virtue* is meaningless until it's applied to the actions of fellow beings, and its effects are seen to be beneficial. What do the words *pain* and *pleasure* mean when one is experiencing neither? The brain recalls times, either positively or negatively, when one or the other was being experienced. But when one hears words like spirituality, immateriality, in-corporeality, etc., the senses and memory cannot help form an idea of their qualities, or of an object with which to connect them. Only a vacuum and emptiness can be formed when contemplating things that are not made of matter, and as such void of qualities. All the errors and disputes of and between mortals have their foundation in the fact that they renounce experience and ignore the evidence of their senses to be guided by notions which they believe to be infused or innate. In reality, these notions are nothing more than the product of over active imaginations and preconceptions, which we have been indoctrinated with since infancy, which habits ingrain, and that authority's mandate. Languages contain many abstract words that are attached to confusing and vague ideas which have no model in Nature.

It is amazing that we frequently use words that cannot be associated with a fixed or precisely determined idea. We endlessly hear about spirits, faculties of the soul, infinity, perfection, virtue, reason, instinct, taste, etc. without being able to tell what is meant by these words. Indeed, even those who use such words cannot define their meaning. Nevertheless, they were invented to falsely represent images of things the senses can experience and the mind can comprehend, appreciate, compare, and judge.

When we think about things that have not acted on our senses we are thinking about words. Since the mind is always trying to attach objects to words, our dreams and imagination fill the void created by these wandering ideas. To give qualities to these objects of the imagination only makes us more arrogant and removes all limits from our ability to error. If we want a word to represent something that has no moving parts but can still act on our organs, which it is impossible to prove its existence or its qualities, the imagination will rack itself to come up with something that might come close to fitting the idea. We come up with images and colors taken from what we already know. So, God has been represented by some as a venerable old man, by others as a powerful ruler, by others as an infuriated and angry being, etc. Obviously, we have served as the model for some of these pictures. But, if we think about an object as a pure spirit that has no body or mass and that is not contained in space, which is beyond nature, at this point we are plunged into emptiness and the mind no longer has any idea or knowledge about that on which it meditates. This is the kind of thinking that was used to create God, and He was frequently annihilated by giving Him incompatible and contradictory attributes. We modeled Him after us by making Him the most moral man while making Him jealous, angry, and vengeful. In doing so He is made inaccessible to the senses because all prior ideas are destroyed and He becomes a mere nothing. From this it appears that those uplifting sciences of Theology & Metaphysics are nothing more than the science of words. Morals and politics, which are frequently mixed with the aforementioned sciences, have consequently become unexplainable mysteries, which can only be exposed through the study of Nature.

We experience truth when we have true relations with others who have a positive influence on our welfare. We know such relations exist only through experience, without which there can be no reason. Without reason we are blind creatures ruled by chance. But how can we gain experience from ideal objects which cannot be known or examined by the senses? How can we be sure of the existence, and know about the qualities, of beings we are not able to feel? How can we be sure that He is working for or against us? Without the proof provided by our senses, how do we know what to love and what to hate, what to pursue and what to avoid, and what to do or not do? Yet this is the confused knowledge upon which so many in the world base their lives. By blending morals, which is the science of relations between people, with vague theological ideas, and weakly basing them on fanciful ideas that exist only in the imagination, the morals that societies depend upon become uncertain, arbitrary, subject to whims, and baseless.

All beings must think differently due to their natural organization, the changes they experience, and the habits they acquire. Our temperament, which undergoes many changes, determines our mental qualities. It follows that each individual's imagination is unique and will create different images than those of other individuals. Each individual is a connected whole which is influenced by its different parts. Different eyes will see the same real objects differently, resulting in different ideas. Imagine how different ideas will be, if the object being discussed cannot be seen by the eyes or experienced by the other senses. People have similar ideas about objects that everyone experiences. But perceptions will never be exactly the same in any two people. So, when people seem to have the same thinking, judgments, passions, desires, tastes, and consent about an idea, their feelings have come to be as a result of different experiences. Words alone cannot describe the different modes of seeing and thinking that have formed individuals with similar views. In a sense, each individual speaks a language that is specific to that person and not completely comprehensible to others. So, how can people agree on objects known only to the imagination? Can the imagination of one ever be the same as that of another? How can they understand each other when they assign qualities to imaginary objects based on the way their minds work? For two individuals to think exactly alike is to insist that they are the same in every way, from physical and mental makeup to their experiences in every moment of their respective lives. If this could happen then all of us would be exactly the same. And are our opinions our own creation or the result of everything we experiences from infancy, which influence the way we think and act? If we are a connected whole, whenever we see a different feature in another being shouldn't we conclude that it is not possible for their brains to think, associate ideas, imagine, or dream in the exact same way? And the differences in the temperament of individuals are the source of the differences in passions, taste, ideas of happiness, and opinions about everything. Unfortunately, these same differences are the fatal source of our disputes, hatred, and injustice every time we try to explain unknown objects to which we attach great importance. We will never understand ourselves or others when trying to explain a spiritual soul or immaterial substances that have no basis in Nature. At that moment we are speaking our own language, attaching our own ideas to words that others interpret differently. How should it be determined as to who is thinking correctly? How does one decide who has the best imagination? Can a balance be found to determine whose knowledge is the most correct when discussing subjects that cannot be observed by the senses, that have no model, and that are above reason? Every individual, legislator, observer, and nation has formed their own ideas about these things. Each believes their specific musings are preferable to those of their neighbors, which always appear to be absurd, ridiculous, and false to others who believe differently. Each clings to their opinions because each believes that their happiness and welfare depend on attachments to their prejudices. Ask a person to change to your religion and you will be viewed as a madman, and no doubt responded to with indignation and contempt. When you are asked to change your religion to the other you will begin to treat each other as absurd beings, ridiculously opinionated, and extremely stubborn. Such discussions frequently start out as light hearted but always become heated disputes when defending matters of importance, passion, and self-love. The participants grow angry and quarrel. Sometimes feelings of hatred surface and the end result is physical injury to one or more. So, because of opinions that no one can demonstrate, we see the Hindu despised, the Muslims hated, and the Pagans held in contempt. Each is oppressed and scorned with the most malicious hatred. Christians burned Jews for clinging to the faith of their fathers. Roman Catholics condemned Protestants to the flame and made a practice of massacring them in cold blood. At one point different Christian sects united to fight the Turks after which they returned to slaughtering each other.

If our imaginations and dreams were the same, the fanciful ideas they put forth would be the same everywhere and there would be no disputes about this subject. Many lives would be saved if we would spend time studying objects that actually exist, and have qualities that can be discovered through true experiences. Systems of Science usually come to agreement because when there is a debate, studies continue until the truth surfaces and errors are detected. Mathematicians usually agree about very complicated topics. Theologians, on the other hand, have such a hard time agreeing among themselves because their beliefs are based on the prejudices they were indoctrinated with since their youth. They are always reasoning, not on real objects, but on objects of their imaginations, which they have never examined in reality. Their arguments are not based on facts and experience, but on meaningless ideas of beings without form. Because these beliefs have been around for such a long time few people challenge them, and most accept them as incontestable truths simply because they've been told they exist. Because great importance is attached to these beliefs, those who have the audacity to doubt or even examine them are viewed with contempt.

If our ancestors had been able to examine their beliefs they would have discovered that many of the objects, which resulted in the most shocking and bloody disputes, were mere phantoms that were not worthy of their efforts. The priests of Apollo would have been harmless if the tenets they proposed would have been closely examined. Followers would have seen that they were cutting their neighbors throats for words that did not make sense. Or, at least they would have learned to doubt their right to act as they did, renouncing the inflexible superior tone they assumed, while convincing their peers to unite with them in thought and action. The slightest amount of reflection would have shown that thoughts and imaginings are a result of Natural development, which influences wills and actions. If they had relied upon morals and reason, everything would have proven that rational beings think differently, yet must live peaceably together and love each other. Whether discussing subjects that are impossible to truly know and there is no agreement, or topics where there is agreement, it's important for there to be a mutual sense of support. All the evidence would have convinced them that the tyranny was, and still is, unreasonable, the violence unjust, and the cruelty of those men of blood who persecute and destroy mankind so they could force their opinions was, and still is, useless. Everything would have conducted mortals to kindness, understanding, and tolerance, unquestionably virtues of more real importance and necessity to the welfare of society than the marvelous speculations that divide and frequently lead to bloodshed and wars with pretended enemies in revered fights of the imagination.

From this, the importance of examining the ideas attached to morals is clear, since we are continually sacrificing our own happiness to destroy the peacefulness of nations at the irrational command of fanatical and cruel leaders. We must start by examining and learning from our experiences, which requires a return to Nature, the use of reason, and the study of objects that are real and useful to our permanent happiness. We must study the laws of Nature and we must study ourselves, to truly know the bonds that unite us with our fellow mortals. We must also study the made-up bonds that chain us to the most harmful beliefs. And if our imaginations must always create illusions that we hang on to and hold dear, then we should allow others to have their own illusions or seek the truth that best suits them, always remembering that all the opinions, ideas, systems, wills, and actions are the necessary consequence of our nature, our temperament, our organization, and the causes, either temporary or constant, that modify us. In short, that we are less free agents to think than to act: a truth that will be proven again in the following chapter.

Chapter 11

The System of Our Free Agency

Those who say the soul is: separate from the body; immaterial; capable of formulating its own ideas; able to act with its own energy and without the aid of external objects; are saying that the soul is empowered to act without adherence to the physical laws that all beings we know of must obey. They believe the soul controls its conduct, regulates its operations, and determines its will by its own natural energy. In a word, they have pretended that we are *free agents*.

It has already been sufficiently proven that the soul is nothing more than the body which continuously changes as the body does. Without the body the soul is inert and dead. Consequently, everything that happens to the soul has a material or physical cause. The development of our intellect and morals can be explained in a purely physical and natural manner. Finally, all the ideas, systems, and opinions, whether true or false, which we form are attributable to our physical interactions with material objects, or our senses. So, however you want to think of our species, we are purely physical beings connected to a universal Nature, and subject to the immutable laws she imposes on all her beings without ever consulting with them. Our life is a line that Nature commands us to follow without ever being able to swerve from it, not even for an instant. Indeed, we are born without our consent, our organization is not our choice, our ideas are given to us, and our habits are the result of our surroundings. We are constantly being changed by concealed or visible causes that we have no control over, which result in the way each individual thinks and acts. We are good or bad, happy or sad, wise or foolish, and reasonable or irrational, without the will moving us toward any of these various states. Nevertheless, despite the shackles that bind us, it is pretended that we are free agents, independent of the real causes that move us. We believe that we determine our will and regulate our condition. And, regardless that everything points to the weakness of this opinion, it is held as an incontestable truth, and even believed to be enlightened thinking. It is the basis of religion, which would not be able to explain whether we were deserving of reward or punishment if we were not free agents. Societies have adopted this belief because, if all of our actions are necessary the right to punish criminals would no longer exist. Over time human vanity gave way to the hypothesis that distinguishes us from all other physical beings, making our actions totally independent of other causes. But truly, the slightest amount of reflection would have shown the absurdity and impossibility of this belief.

We are subordinate to, and obliged to, experience the influence of Nature. If we were free agents then each individual would either be greater than all of Nature or not be part of her at all. But, Nature is always in motion and requires all her beings to act and concur with her general motion. Another way of saying this is she conserves her existence through the beings that exist within her, each of which has particular energies that conform to fixed, eternal, and immutable laws. If we were free agents we would lose our connection with Nature, thereby losing our essence and our physical sensibilities. We would not know good from evil, pleasure from pain, and we would no longer be able to conserve our existence, which is to find happiness. All beings would become indifferent to each other ceasing to know what to love, what to fear, what to seek, and what to avoid. We would be unnatural beings, incapable of acting as we do. It is natural for us to tend to our well-being and want to conserve our existence. This primitive impulse leads to sensations like pain, which warns us as to what we should avoid, and pleasure which show us what we should desire. As such we love those things that excite happiness and hate those things that cause us to feel fear or uneasiness. Therefore, we must necessarily be attracted to objects that we see as advantageous or useful, and reject objects that we see as harmful to our habitual or transitory mode of existence. It is only through experience that we learn what we should love and what we should fear. If our organs are healthy, our experiences will be true. We will display reason, prudence, foresight, and good judgment, knowing that sometimes what we think is good may become evil, and what we view as evil may produce solid and durable good. It is experience that would show us that the amputation of a limb, a physically and psychologically painful procedure, is acceptable if it saves a life and prolongs existence. So we submit to the momentary pain in favor of the long term good.

Will is a change in the brain that puts it or the body into action. Will is determined by the qualities of the object, or motives that acts on the senses, or an idea that is recalled. These qualities can be good or bad and agreeable or painful. Consequently, actions are the necessary result of the impulses received from the motive, the idea, or the object that changes the brain and forms the will. When one does not act according to this impulse it is because a new or different cause, motive, or idea changes the brain and gives a new impulse, suspending the old. So the sight or the idea of an agreeable object causes the will to set us into action to get it. But, if a new and more powerful object or idea comes it can give the will a new direction. This is where reflection, experience, and reason can change the actions of the will. Without this, we would have necessarily followed the first impulse toward a desirable object. In all this we are always acting according to necessary laws that we have no control over.

If, when we are very thirsty, we form an idea that a glass of water will subdue this feverish thirst, are we the masters of ourselves? There is no doubt that we should want to satisfy it, but if we were told the water was poisoned, we would choose not to drink it. At this point it may be falsely concluded that we are free agents. The fact is that the motive, which is self-preservation, is the same in both cases. The desire to conserve one-self either annihilates or suspends the desire to drink and the second motive becomes stronger than the first. The fear of death, or the desire to live, necessarily prevails over the painful sensation caused by the eagerness to drink. And what if the thirst was so great that the decision is made to drink the tainted water? The first motive regains control and the belief that life may be preserved by drinking rules. Nevertheless, whether we drink the water or not, our actions are the necessary result of which ever motive is stronger and consequently creates within us the will to act. This example serves to explain the phenomena of the human will. The will, or the brain, is like a ball which receives an impulse and moves in a straight line until a force superior to the first causes it to change direction. The person who drank the poisoned water appears to be a madman, but the actions of fools are as necessary as those of the most prudent individuals. The motives that cause us to act in ways that are harmful to ourselves or others are as powerful as those which cause wise men to act as they do. In both cases, their actions are necessary, but it will be insisted that the harmful person can be convinced to change actions. This does not make that person a free agent. Instead, sufficiently powerful motives can replace the old ones and form a new will that results in different actions.

We are said to *deliberate* when we think about some choices we are confronted with and suspend the action of the will. We only deliberate when we do not understand the impulses we receive from an object, or we do not have enough experience to predict the effects our actions will create. For example, a person is trying to decide about taking a vacation or staying home. Consequently, the deliberation involves weighing the motives to go against those to stay home. We make the choice that is most probable, removing the indecision as to whether we should go or stay. Our actions are always the immediate or ultimate advantage we find, or think we find, that influence the final decision. Our will frequently wavers between two objects that move us in different directions. But, even in this time of comparing these objects or ideas, we are not free agents for a single instant. The good or evil that we believe we see in the objects, the fears or desires that are excited by our uncertainty, are the necessary motives of our momentary will. Obviously, deliberation and uncertainty are necessary, but whatever the final choice, be it right or wrong, good or bad, we feel it will be to our advantage. When the soul is confronted by two motives that simultaneously move it in different directions, it deliberates. The brain tries to balance the two, at times favoring one and at times favoring the other until one wins which suspends the indecision of the will. But, if the causes are equally strong and moving the brain in different directions, the brain shuts down. It is not able to will or act. It waits until one cause overpowers the other which then gives the will the power to act. This simple and natural mechanism shows why uncertainty is so painful and suspense is always a violent state for us. The brain, an organ so delicate, so mobile, and which experiences very rapid modifications, becomes fatigued when confronted with two causes that move it in different directions. This explains our moments of irregularity and indecision as well as conduct that appear to be an unexplainable mystery. Experience shows us that the soul is subject to the same physical laws as the material body. If the will of each individual, during a given time, was only moved by a single cause or passion, it would be easy to predict actions. But, when confronted by contrary powers, by adverse motives that act on us at the same time or in succession, the brain becomes fatigued or tormented and it shuts down or goes into a state of shock. It is at this time that one might perpetrate criminal acts in spite of the dangers that might accompany the act. It is also the state that might make us feel remorse, preventing us from enjoying the fruits of our criminal actions.

When the powers or causes that act on the mind are opposed, the soul, as well as the body, will take a middle direction between the two. This condition is sometimes painful and leads to a troubled existence, causing us to stop caring about our conservation, and even move us toward our own death as a way to escape from ourselves and our despair. As such, we see individuals who are miserable, discontented, and voluntarily destroy themselves when life becomes unbearable. We can only enjoy existence as long as life holds promise. When we are in continuous pain or torn by contrary impulses, our natural tendency is disturbed and we are compelled to find a new direction. This could move us to contemplate suicide which appears as the most desirable outcome. This explains the actions of those unhappy beings whose vicious temperaments or tortured consciences, whose disappointment and weariness, sometimes cause them to take their own lives. The varied and complicated powers that act, either successively or simultaneously on the brain, that change us in so many ways over the course of our existence, are the true causes of this perplexing conduct. Indeed, this is why it is so hard to explain the confused morals and the true reasons for so many of our actions. The factors that drive us can be compared to a labyrinth, because we rarely possess the necessary gifts to assess them. So it seems that circumstances, indecision, and conduct are the necessary consequences of changes we experience, or the motives that successively form the will, which are dependent on the frequent changes that the mind and body undergo. Interestingly, the same motives don't always have the same effects on the will, and objects that once pleased us don't anymore. As a result, our temperament changes either momentarily or forever. Consequently, taste, desires, passions, and will change. There can be no uniformity in our conduct or any certainty about the effects to be expected. Choice by no means proves the free-agency of an individual. We only deliberate when we do not know which object or idea will work to our advantage. Choice is necessary in order to determine which object, idea, or action will be most advantageous. If we had free-agency we would be able to will, or choose, without motives, or we could prevent motives from influencing our will. But, because actions come about as a result of the will, and the will is formed by motives which we have no power over, it follows that we are never the master of our specific will. Consequently, we never act as free agents. It is thought that we have free will because we have a will and the power to choose. What is being ignored is the fact that our will is formed by causes independent of ourselves, those being a combination of our make-up and our surroundings. Indeed, we live a great part of our life without ever willing. Habitual motives direct the will which result in most of our actions. If we were to count all our actions from the time we awake until the moment we go to sleep, we would find that not one of our actions was voluntary, but instead they were mechanical and habitual, determined by causes that we could not foresee, to which we felt we had to do or were convinced to do. We would discover that we have been seduced or drawn along by motives which necessarily influence all our actions and thoughts. Are you the master of willing to remove your hand from a fire, knowing it will burn you? Or do you have the power to douse the fire so that it will not harm you? Can you choose to eat food that you like and avoid food that does not agree with you? It is always within our make-up that we judge things to be good or bad. But, whatever this judgment, it will depend on how we feel, which can be the result of habitual or accidental actions as well as the qualities we find in the causes that move us, all of which exist without our knowledge or approval.

Before the will is activated we must have causes like sensations, perceptions, or ideas, whether complete or incomplete, whether true or false, that we feel either strongly or weakly. If this was not the case we would make choices without motives. So, to speak correctly, all causes effect the will. No matter how faint an impulse from an object, an image, or an idea, as soon as the will acts, the impulse has been sufficient to move us. The result of a weak impulse is a weakness of will which is known as *indifference*. The brain has difficulty perceiving a weak impulse, and consequently moves with less energy to obtain or remove the object or idea that has modified it. A powerful impulse results in a strong will followed by strong actions to obtain or remove the object that appears to be very agreeable or very troublesome.

We were thought to be free agents because it was imagined that our souls could recall ideas which sometimes served to check unruly desires. As such, the idea of a remote evil frequently prevents us from enjoying a present or actual good. Memory, which is a slight and hardly noticeable change in the brain, constantly destroys the real objects that act upon the will. We do not choose the ideas that we recall, nor do we control how or to what they associate. They are arranged where they have made more or less profound impressions, despite us and without our knowledge. Our memory depends on our organization. Its fidelity depends on the habitual or momentary state in which we find ourselves. When our will is formed by a strong motive that excites a great passion, we move after the attainment of the object aggressively, not able to sense the cautionary objects or ideas that might point out the dangers of our actions. We no longer judge soundly and cannot foresee the consequences of our actions. We are not able to apply our experiences to the situation or use reason. Natural operations of the brain allow us to think clearly, but when in a state of delirium it loses all capacity to do so.

The way one thinks is determined by the person and must therefore depend on the individual's natural organization, and the changes that take place independent of the will. From this it is clear that our thoughts, reflections, manner of viewing things, feelings, judgments, and the way we combine ideas are neither voluntary nor free. The soul is not capable of creating motion or creating ideas to counter impulses it receives. This is why we are not able to reason when in a state of passion. At that moment we are comparable to someone experiencing a state of ecstasy or drunkenness. Wicked people are always either drunk or mad, not able to reason until they return to a state of tranquility. Once capable of seeing the evil they have done people who are not psychopaths or sociopaths experience *shame, regret,* and *remorse.*

The mistaken belief that the will is the original motive for our actions is how the idea of the free agency came about. Because we could not or would not look back, we could not see the multitude of complicated causes which, independent of us, change the brain to form the will. Through all this we are purely passive regarding the motions we receive. Can we choose to desire or not desire an object that appears desirable? The answer is an unequivocal NO. Are we the masters of resisting desire if we think about the consequences? Yes, but can we think about consequences when the soul is consumed by a very strong passion, one which depends on our natural organization and the causes that formed us? Can we give the consequences enough meaning that they will counter our passion? Are we the masters of making something we find desirable to no longer have the qualities that we desire? We are told that we should learn to resist our passions and curb our desires. Of course we should, but are we capable of doing so? Does one's temperament, imagination, and physical makeup enable, or permit, the use of true experience at the moment it's wanted? It must also be asked if one's education, and the examples and ideas that were inspirations in early life helped form the habit of repressing desires. In reality, all these things have contributed to make us seek with passion and desire the objects which you say we ought to resist. Indeed, the *ambitious person* cries out, "You want me to resist my passions? Yet these passions were ingrained within me from the moment of birth." Frequently they become the source of unchecked power and the envy of others, all to the detriment of the majority within a society. The *miser* says, "You forbid me to love money and seek the means of acquiring it, but what you really ask is for me to change the person I am!" Certainly money is needed to survive and achieve a certain degree of happiness, but we see billionaires and large corporations resort to the most unscrupulous means to obtain wealth. The hedonist argues, "Was I the maker of my own temperament, which unceasingly invites me to pleasure?" Yet in the world we live in some people are proud of their over indulgences and rewarded for them. The angry person feels that disposition is natural and it is the only way to atone for the injuries received. And the religious zealot thinks he is doing God's work when judging or harming others who do not think the way he does. Our actions are never free, but always the result of our temperament, of the ideas we have received, of our belief about how to attain happiness, be it right or wrong, and of our opinions, which are strengthened by example, education, and experience. So much of what we experience, from the superstitions we learn, to our governments, to our education, set examples before us that push us toward evil and a morality that tries to teach us virtue is in vain. In societies where vice, crime, and corruption are rewarded for some and severely punished for others, virtue is a meaningless word. In the two-tiered justice system the wealthiest commit unspeakable crimes and walk free, while the poorest are killed and incarcerated at alarming rates.

So, you are not a free agent at any one moment of your life. You are guided in every action by the real or fictitious advantages that you give to objects that arouse your passions. These passions are a necessary part of any being who is always striving toward happiness. The energy one expends toward passions is a consequence of that person's temperament, which is formed by the physical elements that make us who we are. Changes to our temperament are the inevitable consequence of impulses we get from moral and physical beings.

A mind that is clear of prejudice can plainly see that we have no free agency, yet if one were to insist with a small feeling of triumph that he could choose to move or not move his hand, an action referred to as *indifferent*, it would appear that this person is the master of choosing, and therefore a free agent. The reply is that this is a perfectly simple example of a person performing an action which he is resolved on doing, and does not prove free agency. The desire of displaying the quality, excited by a dispute, becomes the motive that pushes the will to do one or the other. What he does not see at this moment is the true motive that sets him into action, which is the desire to convince his opponent. If, in the heat of the discussion he were to ask, "Is it my choice to throw myself out the window?" I would answer no. As a reasonable being there is no way he would end his life to prove the point of his free agency. And even if he were to jump, it would not mean that he was a free agent, but it was his violent temperament that led him to it. Madness depends on many factors but the will is not one of them. A fanatic or a hero will brave death just as a coward will run from it. There is no difference between a person who is thrown out of a window and one who jumps, except the impulse in the first comes from an outside source and in the second it comes from within. Both have exterior causes with the second not being as clear as the first might appear to be. When someone holds his hand in a fire, he is acting out of necessity caused by interior motives that led him to this strange action as if his arm were being forcibly held there. Pride, despair, the desire to be braver than his enemies, the wish to astonish or intimidate, etc. were the chains that held his hand bound to the fire. The love of glory or patriotism or the wish to astonish has led others to perform such acts throughout the history of mankind.

We are thought to be free agents because there are times when we overcome all obstacles to reach a desired goal. The reply to this line of thinking is that we have no control over placing or removing the obstacles we encounter. The motives that move us to action do not come from our own power whether the motives comes from exterior or internal objects. We are not master of the thoughts, which always come from causes independent of us and that determine our will.

To understand the truth about the system of free agency, and no longer be deceived, all one has to do is look back to the motives that form the will. We will always find that these motives are out of our control. It is believed that when an idea comes to the mind, consequently we act freely if no obstacles stop us. The question is how did the idea originate in the brain? Do we have the power of preventing it and not having the idea again? Does the idea come from exterior objects that modify the brain without our knowledge or approval? Can we prevent our eyes from seeing an object and sending an idea of the object to the brain, and changing the brain. We are not master of the obstacles we encounter, which are the necessary effects of either interior or exterior causes, which always act according to their given properties. If a coward is insulted by someone he will not respond to the insult, even though he would like to, because his will cannot overcome his cowardice. The fact that he is a coward is a result of his natural development and does not depend on him. In this case the coward is insulted and must endure it, all against his will.

Those who believe in a system of free agency always seem to confuse limitations with necessity. We think we act as free agents every time we choose an action and there are no obstacles to limit us. We do not see that the motive that causes us to will is necessary and never a choice that we make. A prisoner in solitary confinement must remain in jail, but is not a free agent. He wishes to escape but his cell prevents him from doing so, however it does not prevent him from willing. He would leave his cell if he could but he would not do so as a free agent. Fear of punishment or desire for freedom would be sufficient motives for his actions. When we act without restraint it does not make us a free agent. All our actions are necessary and based on motives that make us who we are, and over which we have no control. We are like a heavy body that finds itself in a free fall that will either gravitate or continue to fall. But who would say that this dense body is free to fall or not? Its descent is the necessary effect of its own unique gravity. The virtuous Socrates submitted to the laws of his country, even though they were unjust, and although he could have avoided prison he would not save himself. But even here he did not act as a free agent. The invisible chains of opinion, the secret love of dignity, the inward respect for the laws even when they were unjust, and the fear of ruining his reputation kept him in prison. These motives were powerful enough to cause this virtuous man to await death with tranquility. It was not in his power to save himself because he could not find a motive strong enough to make him let go of the principles to which his mind had grown accustom.

We have falsely concluded that we are free agents because we occasionally act against our feelings. However, when we act against our feelings there is always a motive strong enough to overcome those feelings.

A sick man who sees his cure as a series of very unpleasant procedures uses necessary and intelligent motives such as fear of pain or death to make his final decisions. Consequently, we cannot truly say this sick man is acting freely.

When we say we are not free agents, we do not mean to compare ourselves to a body that is moved by a simple impulsive cause. We contain causes within us that are dependent on our past. We have a very complex brain that gets its ideas from perceptions that are formed by sensations it receives from outside objects. How these sensations and perceptions engrave ideas on the brain is far too complicated for us to know. Because we cannot see the chain of events that move us, in essence the motive-principle that acts within us, we think we are free agents. Literally translated, we think that we move ourselves by ourselves and make decisions without cause. In reality we should admit that we are ignorant of how or why we act the way we do. Since the soul is the entire being, it cannot act on its own. It must have a motive or a cause to put it into motion. We believe we are free agents because of the many causes that result in all of our actions. If all of our actions were simple and the causes that move us could easily be seen, we would see that all of our actions are necessary because we would instantly see the reasons for our actions. A person who must act a certain way would do so and feel fine about not being a free agent. If we had a sixth sense our actions and the reasons for them would be much more complicated, and we would feel that we are more of a free agent than we are with five senses. So, it is because we cannot recall, analyze, and understand the causes that move us that we believe ourselves to be free agents. Beliefs based on ignorance and deceits are used as proof of this pretended freedom of action. If we could study our actions for a short period of time we would see that the idea of free agency is an illusion that must be destroyed by experience as quickly as possible.

None the less, it must be admitted that the many diverse causes that continually act on us, frequently without our knowledge, make it difficult if not impossible for us to realize the true causes for our actions, let alone those of others. In many cases the causes are so far removed from their effects that when examined there appears to be no relation at all and can only be brought to light as a result of great wisdom. This is why the study of the moral human is so difficult. This is why we cannot fathom the depth of our feelings. We must try to understand the general and necessary laws that control our feelings and actions. For our species these laws are pretty nearly the same with only slight variations, yet their effects cannot be exactly the same in any two individuals. So, as a result of our natural organization, we are always striving to conserve ourselves and to live a happy life. If you refer back to the first of these principles, which is a necessary tendency of the will, we will never be deceived about our motives. But a person without the ability to reason and who is lacking in experience frequently is deceived as to the motives for personal actions. Sometimes ones actions are harmful to others or ones-self, but they are always moving this individual toward an existing or imaginary happiness. These actions are meant to preserve existence based on the current state of thinking and feeling, which can be long term or temporary. Many moral philosophers who did not understand this truth have attributed our actions to fictitious causes and failed to look for the necessary motives for our actions. Politicians and legislators live in the same state of ignorance, or are impostor's who find it easier to use imaginary motive-powers than those that really exist. They would rather have us tremble with the fear of unreal phantoms than guide us to virtue by the direct road to happiness, which is the direction our natural tendencies are always striving toward. It is so true that *error can never possibly be useful to the human species*. Regardless of how true this may be, we either see, or believe we see, the necessary relations of effects and causes in natural philosophy rather than in our own feelings and experiences. At least we see that sensible causes always produce the same effects when circumstances are the same. At this point we stop viewing physical effects as necessary and refuse to recognize the necessity of acts of the human will. Without any kind of proof we give credit for such acts to a motive-power that acts independently, with its own unique energy, capable of modifying itself without the help of exterior causes, and which is distinguished from all material or physical beings. *Agriculture* is based on the experience that the earth can be cultivated and sown to provide grains, fruits, and flowers that are necessary for existence or pleasing to the senses. The *agriculture of the mind* can be thought of in a similar manner. The seeds sown and nurtured will mature to produce either virtue or vice. *Moral fruit* that will either benefit mankind or be a bane to society is nurtured and harvested. *Morals* are the science of relations that exist between the minds, the wills, and the actions of mortals. Just as *geometry* is the science of the relations that exist between bodies, morals would be nothing if it was not based on knowledge of the motives which must necessarily have an influence on the human will, and which must necessarily determine the actions of human beings.

If the moral world was like the physical world, where an uninterrupted cause leads to a necessary effect, it follows that if a *reasonable education*, based on truth and wise laws were instilled during youth, and all forms of good actions were recognized and rewarded, and all forms of actions that hurt the greater whole were put to trial and punished, such actions would affect the will of citizens. The majority of society would see virtue and love as good qualities and the surest road to the happiness each individual so passionately desires. On the other hand, if superstition, politics, example, and public opinion all work to: create evil and train us to be vicious; render our education useless or detrimental; indoctrinate us with false ideas instead of truth; fill the mind with dangerous opinions instead of ideas drawn from experience; turn our passions toward harming ourselves and others instead of kindness and patience; then the majority will follow a path toward evil actions and be a bane to society. The importance of a good education is essential if the mind is to develop in a positive way. Unfortunately a good education is not just incompatible with a system based on superstitions, it's impossible since this does nothing but give the mind a false bias. Such systems work well for arbitrary governments that fear an enlightened populace and prefer the masses to be servants who are mean, contemptible, and afraid. The laws in such societies are based on injustice instead of equity. Customs are followed that oppose common sense and public opinion rejects virtue. Above all, good education is impossible if the teachers have weak minds and only teach the same false ideas that infect them. This is undoubtedly the real source of the widespread depravity and corruption that exists within our society. The politicians and clergy acknowledge the evil but want us to believe the cause is that human nature is corrupt. They blame us for loving ourselves too much and for seeking after our own happiness, insisting we must have supernatural assistance, some marvelous assistance, before we can be good. This harmful doctrine works against our true happiness because it teaches us to believe that we are bad. It discourages us, which leads to a state of laziness or hopelessness while we wait to be enlightened. How could we know that we would always have it if we were well educated and honestly governed? There cannot be a wilder or stranger system of morals than that of Christians who attribute all moral evil to an original sin, and all moral good to the pardon of it. The uselessness of such a system should come as no surprise. What can reasonably be expected as the result of this hypothesis? And in spite of the supposed free agency of humans, they insist only God himself can destroy the wicked desires in the hearts of mortals. Yet no power, whatever, is strong enough to resist the fatal motives that continually affect our will to strive for the attainment of our natural passions. Can't they be seen as inherent in our nature, and doesn't experience show them to be useful since their objective is to avoid injury and obtain anything that is advantageous to our existence? It is easy to see that well-directed passions, when directed toward truly useful objects that are interesting and contribute to the happiness of others, will necessarily contribute to the substantial and permanent well-being of society. Theologians themselves have acknowledged the necessity of passions stating "the passions of man are like a fire, at once necessary to the wants of life, suitable to enhance the condition of humanity, and equally capable of producing the most terrible ravages, the most frightful devastation."

Every experience becomes an impulse to the will. In many cases a single word is enough to change a person for life, permanently modifying preferences. A baby who burns a finger by putting it too close to a flame knows to resist a similar temptation. A person who is punished and despised for committing a crime is, for the most part, not tempted to repeat the actions that caused such discomfort. No matter what stage of development a human is experiencing, we always act based on the impulses given to our will, be it the will of others or by more noticeable physical causes. The nature of the impulse is determined by the nature of the individual. Likes tend to attract each other. Inflamed and fiery imaginations easily influence strong passions. Imaginations that are easily influenced are easy prey for great enthusiasm. The passing of superstitions from generation to generation, the religious errors that move from race to race, and the ease with which we accept the marvelous, are effects that are as necessary as the actions and re-actions created by moving bodies.

All of our actions are based on necessity, despite the useless ideas we have formed about our pretended free-agency, and in defiance of the illusion of this supposed intimate sense. Contrary to our experiences, we are convinced that we are masters of our will. Experience shows us that there is no speculation about this. If certain motives don't have the power required to determine our will, or to stop the progress of our passion, then what use would the ability to speak serve? If we cannot direct our passions toward an end, what good could come from education itself? What does education do if not give the first impulses to the human will, making us form habits and giving us motives, be they true or false, to guide our actions for life? When a father threatens his son with punishment or promises him a reward, doesn't he believe these things will affect his will? Isn't legislation supposed to encourage actions deemed worthy by the majority and discourage harmful actions? The object of morals should be to show us the benefit of suppressing the momentary drive of our passions to promote a more certain happiness and a more lasting well-being. Yet all religions suppose the human race, and all of Nature, must submit to the seductive will of a necessary being, which regulates their condition based on eternal laws and unchallengeable wisdom. Isn't God the absolute master of our destiny, and the divine being who chooses and rejects? The abominations ranted by religions, the promises they put forth, aren't they based on the effects they will necessarily have on mankind? Aren't we brought into existence without our knowledge, and aren't we forced to play a part against our will, and doesn't our happiness or misery depend on the part we play? Indeed, it seems that all religions have *Fatalism* as a foundation. The Greeks punished men for crimes that were predicted by oracles. Theologians have a rather curious defense of the doctrine of free-agency when so many doctrines they believe, *the fall of angels, original sin, etc.* support and are good arguments for a *true system of fatalism*. Yet they teach that *predestination* is a false and dangerous belief that is irreconcilable with Christianity.

Education is viewed as necessary for children. *Legislation* is viewed as necessary for a society to function. *Morals* are the necessary relationships existing between reasonable beings. We view *necessity* as essential regarding all things with which we believe we have certain and unerring experience. We call it *probability* when we do not see a necessary connection between causes and their effects. We would not act as we do if we were not convinced, or at least think we were convinced, that certain effects will necessarily come about as a result of our actions. The *moralist* talks about reason believing it is necessary. The *philosopher* writes believing truth must, sooner or later, prevail over falsehood. *Tyrants* and *fanatical priests* necessarily hate truth and despise reason, because they believe them to be contrary to their interests. The legislators who put into place severe punishments for crimes that they themselves can easily commit without any consequences, do so to keep the populace afraid and controllable. All come to terms with the power, or the necessity, of the motives they use. Each individual flatters ones-self, with or without reason, that these motives will have an influence on the conduct of mankind. Because education is controlled by biases, it is defective and not able to produce the desired effects. And even when education is good, it is quickly countered by everything that takes place in society. Legislation and politics are very frequently evil, serving no purpose but to inflame our passions to the point where they can't be restrained. The great art of the moralist should be to point out and to convince those who are entrusted with the sacred job of regulating the will of the people that their reciprocal happiness depends on the harmony of their passions. The safety, power, and duration of empires necessarily depends on the good senses dispersed among the individual members, the truth of ideas instilled in the minds of citizens, the moral goodness that is nurtured in their hearts, and the virtues that are cultivated in their minds. Religions should be banished unless they truly fortify and strengthen these motives. Unfortunately, in the miserable state that error has plunged a large portion of the human species into, we, for the most part, are seduced to be wicked. We injure our fellow creatures as a matter of conscience because we are taught that persecution is a strong and acceptable motive. Our institutions encourage us to commit evil acts under the lure of promoting our own immediate happiness. In most countries superstition renders people as useless beings, abject slaves who tremble under its terrors, or it turns some into furious fanatics who are cruel, intolerant, and inhuman. In many states arbitrary powers crush we the people, obliging us to become cringing yes men, and making us completely vicious. In those repressive states crimes are rarely punished except for those who are too weak to fight back, or when violent actions that bad government gives birth to can no longer be stopped. Education is neglected and a prudent culture of the mind is despised. Instead, education and culture are dependent upon the bigoted and superstitious priests who are interested in deceiving us and who are sometimes impostors. Our education and culture are dependent on parents and teachers who have no morals and teach their youth the vices with which they are tormented. They teach false opinions which they believe they have an interest in making young minds embrace.

For us to correct the error of our ways we must first understand the source of our original errors. It would be useless to dream about correcting our mistakes and curing our depraved beliefs until the true causes that move the will are exposed. More real, beneficial, and certain motives must be substituted for those which are useless and dangerous to both society and individuals. It is up to those who can influence the human will, those who lead nations and have our real happiness in their grasp, to influence motives using reason and experience as guides. Even something as simple as a good book can touch the hearts of good leaders and become a powerful influence over the conduct of a society or a nation, thereby have an effect on the happiness of a portion of the human race.

We have shown in this chapter that at no one moment of our existence are we free agents. It is Nature that makes us who we are both physically and mentally. Our ideas, which are changes to the brain, are out of our control and instead due to causes that are constantly acting on us, frequently without our knowledge. We are not the master of choosing the things that we enjoy, or wanting things that we desire. We can't control that fact that we deliberate when we are not certain about the effects an object will have on us, and we can't help choosing that which we believe will be most advantageous. The moment our will is determined by our choice we are not able to act in a way other than we do. So, when are we the masters of our own actions? In what moment are we free agents? When we are about to do something it is always a result of what we were, what we are, and everything we had done up to the moment of the action. Our total and actual existence, when viewed under all its possible circumstances, contains the sum of all the motives to the action we are about to commit. The truth of this principle is one which no thinking human being can refute. Our conduct, whether good or bad, virtuous or vicious, useful or prejudicial, either to ones-self or to others, is the succession of actions, a chain of causes and effects, as necessary as all the moments of our existence. To *live*, is to exist in a necessary mode which has a beginning and an end, and which is nothing more than a series of causes and effects. To *will* is to concede or change. To be *free* is to give in to the necessary motives that we carry within us.

If we understood how our organs work and were able to recall all the impulses they have received, all the changes they experienced, and all the effects they have produced, we would know that all our actions are subject to the fate that regulates our own particular system, as it does the entire system of the universe. No effect in a human being, as in Nature, is produced by *chance*, a word which makes no sense. Everything that happens to us and all that we do, as well as all that happens in Nature, or is attributed to her, is a result of necessary laws, which produce necessary effects, from which necessarily flow others. Fate is the eternal, undeniable and necessary order established in Nature. It is the required connection of causes that act with the effects they create. Conforming to this order, heavy bodies fall and light bodies rise, like forms of matter attract while opposites repel, and we congregate in society influencing our fellow beings to become either good or bad, happy or miserable, loving our neighbors or hating them, all based on interactions with each other. As such, we can say that the same necessity that regulates the physical world also regulates the moral world, where everything submits to fate. As we proceed, frequently without our knowledge and despite ourselves, through the life that Nature has put before us, we are like a swimmer who must go with the current that carries him. He thinks he is a free agent because sometimes he consents and sometime he does not consent to go with the flow of the current. None the less, the current is always moving him forward. He thinks he is master of his condition because he must use his arms for fear of sinking. The false ideas he has developed about free-agency, are based on the idea that certain events are judged to be *necessary*, either because he sees an effect that is undeniably linked to a cause, or he believes he has discovered the chain of causes and effects that produce an event. He views other events as *contingent* when he cannot determine the cause for an effect he experiences. Regardless, in Nature everything is connected by the common bond that there is no effect without a cause. In the moral world as well as the physical world, everything happens as a necessary consequence of causes that are either visible or concealed, and must act as they do. *In humans, free-agency is nothing more than necessity contained within us.*

Chapter 12

Is The System of Fatalism Dangerous?

For beings who are constantly working toward their own conservation and happiness, experience is essential. Without it we cannot discover truth, which is nothing more than knowledge of the constant relationships that exist between us and the objects that act on us. Based on our experiences we classify those that contribute to our permanent welfare as useful and valuable. Those that bring somewhat lasting pleasure we call agreeable. Truth becomes useful when we think it will help us, and it becomes dreadful when we think it will injure us. But can the truth actually injure us? Can evil result from a correct understanding of our interactions with other beings? Can our knowledge and understanding of the things we seek in order to bring about happiness be harmful? The answer is NO, unquestionably not. Because truth is *useful* it is valuable. Even when it appears to be disagreeable and contrary to the interests of an individual, it will always be beneficial in the end. It will always benefit the human species as a whole and eternally benefit the great bulk of mankind, who must distance themselves from those who believe it is advantageous for them to lead others into a life of error. *Usefulness,* then, is the cornerstone of our systems, the test of our opinions, and the criteria for our actions. It is why we must value and love truth itself. The most useful truths are the most admirable. Truths which are the most interesting we call *important.* Truths with different meanings that do not correspond to us we call *unproductive.* It is based on this standard that the principles of this book should be judged. Those who are acquainted with all the problems on earth that are created by the erroneous systems of superstition will attest to the importance of opposing them with systems drawn from Nature and based on truth and experience. Those who believe, or say they believe, in maintaining the established system of errors, will view, with horror, the truths presented here. Those obsessed mortals who do not feel the enormous load of misery that mankind experiences due to spiritual speculation, the heavy weight of slavery that makes us groan, will regard all our principles as useless, or the sterile truths that some small numbers of people create to pass time. The wide range of opinions that people have should come as no surprise since no two individuals are ever exactly alike.

As such, based on the ideas of each individual, objects are thought to be useful or useless. So, looking through the eyes of an unbiased and sensible person who values truth, let's examine the *doctrine of fatalism* as useful or dangerous. Is it mere speculation that has no influence over the happiness of the human race? It has already been shown that it gives morals useful arguments to determine the will, and it gives politics the tools it needs to raise the levels of critical thinking within a society. It will also be shown how this doctrine can be used to explain, in a simple way, the mechanics of the actions of humans and the good that we can do. On the other hand, if ideas are the result of fruitless speculation they cannot contribute to the happiness of the human species. Whether one believes we are a free agent or whether one acknowledges the necessity of things, we always move in the direction of our natural tendencies, which are to preserve our existence and live a happy life. A good education, honest habits, wise systems, equitable laws, rewards for good deeds, and just punishments for evil actions will lead us to happiness by making us virtuous. Ridiculous speculations that are full of difficulties can only have influence over people who do not think for themselves. After reflecting on these truths it will be easy to see beyond the problems associated with the system of fatalism. Many people, who cannot see beyond their superstitions and prejudices, would have you believe that a belief in fatalism is dangerous. They want you to think such a belief is meant to disturb public peace, challenge the opinions that we ought to have, and confuse our perceptions of vice and virtue.

Those who oppose the idea of the necessity of our actions say that if that were the case, then no one would have the right to punish bad actions or even be angry with those who commit them. They contend that laws would be unjust if they punished necessary actions. Such a system could never have merit or imperfection. In response, it can be argued that to accredit an action to anyone is to acknowledge that person as the author of that action. But, the accusation would be a lie since the good or bad effects given to an action are ideas that originate as a result of its effects on those who experience it. If we concede that the agent is necessary, we still are not sure if the effects are good or bad to those who must feel its influence. Actions, all of which are necessary, produce either feelings of love or anger. Love and anger are emotions that can result in changes to human beings. When we inflict punishments on our fellow beings we are trying to deter an individual from committing displeasing acts. As such, anger is a necessary result of Nature, and the consequence of our temperament. The pain caused by a stone that falls on the arm does not hurt any less because it comes from a cause that has no will, but acts by the necessity of its Nature. While thinking about our actions as necessary, it's impossible to avoid differentiating between actions that have a positive effect and those that are negative, which Nature requires us to take responsibility for and to stop. From this it can be seen that the system of fatalism does not in any way change the state of things and is not meant to confuse ideas of vice and virtue.

Our Nature always rejects things that go against it. There are people who get so angry that they become infuriated with insensible and inanimate objects. Reflecting on their inability to change these objects should bring them back to their senses. Parents frequently become angry with their children who are not fully developed or have been poorly taught. Nothing is more common in life than to see people and societies punish fellow beings for faults of which they are the cause. Laws are made so that societies can endure by preventing us from harming our neighbors. Such laws punish those who disturb societal harmony by injuring others. Whether such people are acting out of necessity or as free agents, it is important to know that their actions can be modified and are therefore subject to the laws. Severe laws are, or should be, implemented to control the passions that cause some to act in ways that are harmful to individuals and to society as a whole. Punishment must be suitable to the crime and nothing more. When such a balance is not maintained the foundations of the legal system and the society deteriorate. Whatever causes us to act the way we do, society has the right to crush effects deemed detrimental to it. Just as a person whose land would be ruined by a river has the right to build banks or change the course of the river, if possible, in order to save the land. Because of this right, society has the power to create laws and enforce them with appropriate punishments for those who may be tempted to commit, or who commit, acts that threaten the peace, security, and happiness within it.

It is thought that society should only punish acts that are products of free will, and the nature of the crime, the degree of its brutality, is determined by the will of the perpetrator. As such, if there is no free will, no crime should be punished. I reply that society is an assemblage of sensible and reasonable people who fear evil and seek after good and their own welfare. These feelings allow for the will to be changed in order to bring about the desired end results. Education, the laws, public opinion, example, habit, and fear are the tools that society uses to change the will so that passions are regulated and actions are restrained. The results are the general happiness of the majority, making an impression on every person whose organization, essence, and sanity allow each individual to form new habits and thoughts, and as such is inspired by society. Fear of punishment, or loss of happiness, can and should be used to influence the will of individuals, and therefore regulate actions. Those who cannot change their actions and passions and who present a threat to their fellow beings are not fit to live in a society. The individual who goes against the interests of fellow citizens should be subject to the law, which is, or should be, an expression of the general will. The unsociable individual who experiences punishments that fit the crime will, hopefully, experience personal changes in motivations and therefore the will. If society has the right to preserve itself, it has the right to enforce laws that should influence the will of people with motives that will deter us from committing actions that cause injury. If the motives are not sufficient to stop the harmful actions of an individual or a group of individuals, society must, for its own preservation, take away the power to do more harm. Whatever the reason for the injurious actions, be it free-will or necessity, if society has provided motives that work with reasonable beings, yet don't work for some, it must take action with these depraved individuals. Society has the right to punish individuals who are truly injurious to her, if she has provided the motives to influence the will of the majority. Society does not have the right to punish if the law has failed to provide motives necessary to influence the will, and that society has not provided the means for each individual to work, enjoy life, and contribute to the community. It is unjust to punish those who were deprived a good education, or not taught honest principles, or who were not given the chance to form habits needed to be a contributing member of society. The law is defective when crimes are a result of flaws within the society, and punishments are not in alignment with crimes. The last degree of injustice, the height of folly is, when society is so blinded that it punishes citizens who have served it usefully.

Laws and penalties should present to the members of a society, who respond to fear of punishment, motives that will influence the will. The idea of pain, loss of liberty, and fear of death are, to reasonable beings who want to enjoy life, very strong motives that should deter them from giving in to desires that are harmful. If the will is not changed by such motivations, then you are dealing with a mad, irrational being who is not well adjusted and who society must protect itself against. Madness is, without doubt, an involuntary and necessary state. No one feels it is unjust to deprive the insane of freedoms even though their actions are a result of a deranged mind. Wicked people are those whose brains are either constantly or occasionally disturbed. Still, they must be punished or restrained as a response to the evil acts they commit. They must be stopped from injuring until they can return to society and function productively. If they cannot conform to the rules of a society, they must permanently be excluded from its benefits. And it should not be necessary to examine the punishments society imposes on those who break the laws if they are reasonable and work toward the conservation of society. The system of fatalism, as we have seen, does not leave crime unpunished, but it is at least intended to control the cruelty and extreme anger that some nations use to punish victims. This cruelty becomes even more absurd, when experience shows it to be ineffective. The habit of witnessing brutal punishments familiarizes criminals with the idea. If it is true that society has the right to take the life of one of its members, that the death of a criminal would be advantageous to society, an idea that must be examined, humanity requires that the death should not include torture. Too frequently such rigorous laws are created by disturbed leaders who seem to delight in overwhelming their victims. Such cruelty defeats its own end when it makes the criminal, who is being submitted to public revenge, suffer without any advantage to society. It moves the compassion of the spectator to the side of the miserable offender who groans under the weight of the punishment. And it does nothing to change the wicked but show them the cruelties that they will have to endure, which frequently makes them more violent, cruel, and more the enemy of society. If the penalty of death was not used at all, or at least used less frequently and without torture, it might be more effective. Experience seems to show that the criminal, or victim, views death as *a bad quarter of an hour*. It is an unquestionable fact, that a thief who sees a comrade break-down under punishment might say, "*How many times have I told you, that in our business, we have committed one more evil than the rest of mankind?*" Crimes are committed in spite of the punishments inflicted by society. In nations that use the death penalty freely, is any thought ever given to the great number of individuals who would be able to render very useful service to pay their debt to society for the crimes committed. The ease with which lives are taken is a reflection of the values of the society. It shows an unwillingness to provide counseling and is proof of the negligence of law-makers, who find it easier to destroy a life then find ways to make them better.

And what can be said about the unjust cruelty of nations who make laws that should benefit the whole of society but in reality only serve the needs of the powerful? How can we defend the inhumanity of societies where punishments don't even come close to fitting the crime, and lives are unmercifully ended when some unfortunate beings commit crimes to survive in a land of plenty? In many civilized nations the life of a citizen is valued in the same way as money or property. The homeless person is condemned to prison, and sometimes death, for stealing from those with abundance in order to survive. In many enlightened societies this is called *justice*, or making the punishment fit the crime. All, *the humanitarian* who feels for the welfare of fellow beings, *the moralist* who speaks of virtue, *the philosopher* who studied the secrets of Nature, and even *the theologian*, should declare this dreadful iniquity a heinous sin, especially since the tortures and the crimes are the product of irrational customs, exaggerated by bad institutions, and multiplied by evil examples. Isn't this like building a cheap hotel then punishing the inhabitants for staying there because it's not a four star resort? It cannot be said often enough that we are prone to evil because everything we see and experience seems to push us in that direction, and frequently we see vice win over good. Education is lacking or defective in some if not all cases. In most societies the principles we see and learn, along with those provided by an unintelligible superstition, are encouraged by corrupt examples. The law tells us not to steal from our neighbors, but more powerful wants tell us we must live. Unaccustomed to reason and discipline we think we must commit crimes at the expense of a society that has done nothing for us. If we do not have the basic necessities to survive, which our essence requires us to seek and we are not the master of, then we will try to acquire those necessities in any way possible. We plunge ourselves into a life of crime, resorting to theft and murder as a way of living, all to satisfy the wants, be they real or imaginary, which everything around us conspires to create. Deprived of a proper education, we have not learned how to restrain the fury of our temperament and guide our passions with discretion or curb our feelings. Without ideas of decency and lacking the true principles of honor, we engage in criminal activities that harm the country, which has been nothing more than a step-mother to us. In a fit of rage, our deranged mind loses sight of our neighbor's rights. Overlooking the consequences of punishment and torture, unruly desires which have become too strong set us on a path of criminal actions. Our actions become habits which over time become unchangeable. Laziness makes us apathetic, remorse disturbs our peace, despair leaves us blind, and so we rush on to death. Society must punish actions which, in many cases, it has produced in the hearts and minds of citizens by evil examples, or which at least, it has not taken the pains to try and root out by providing suitable motives that would lead to honest principles, industrious habits, and virtuous inclinations. So, society frequently punishes those crimes of which it is itself the author, or which its negligence has created in the minds of its members. It is like the unjust father who punishes his child for vices learned from him.

However unjust and unreasonable this conduct may be, it is none the less necessary. Whatever corruption and vices a society and its institutions may exhibit, like everything in Nature, they must exist. Consequently, society is obliged to punish the excesses that it has produced. Despite its prejudices and vices it feels strongly that it must stop the actions of those who threaten its tranquility, because it is always striving for its own conservation. As such, society removes obstacles and even punishes some with more or less passion depending on the importance it places on the objects, or what it sees as most suitable to further its own welfare. And even though society frequently deceives itself with regards to its problems and the correct solutions, it deceives itself necessarily as it strives for knowledge calculated to enlighten it with regards to its true interests. It desires leaders who exhibit the required virtues of regulating its movements via vigilance and suitable talents. From this it appears that the injustices within a poorly organized society are as necessary as the crimes of those who attack it with vice and hostility. When the body politic is in a state of insanity it cannot act with reason any more than one of its members whose brain is disturbed with madness.

It must appear that submitting everything to necessity confuses, or even destroys, the notions we have of justice and injustice, good and evil, and merit and disadvantage. I don't agree. Although everything we do is necessary, our actions are good and just when they work toward the real unity of all within the society of which we are a part. They are necessarily different from actions meant to harm our fellow beings. Society is just, good, and deserving of our respect when it provides for the physical needs of its members, as well as affording them protection, liberty, and puts them in possession of their natural rights. Without these the happiness of a society is vulnerable. Society is unjust, bad, and not worthy of our esteem when it is partial to a few and cruel to many. It is then that its enemies grow in number and those enemies seek vengeance via criminal actions, which must be punished. True notions of justice and injustice are not dependent on the whims of a political society. The right ideas of moral good and evil, and the just appreciation of merit and fault, depend on *utility*, which is the necessity of things, which always forces us to act as we do and feel a sense of approval or disdain for everything we experience. In some instances we cannot help but approve of our actions, as well as those of fellow beings and of society. At other times we cannot approve of certain actions and are even compelled to hate or condemn them. We base our ideas of pain and pleasure, right and wrong, and vice and virtue on our own unique organization. The only difference between these is that we are instantly aware of the sensations of pleasure and pain. On the other hand, frequently the benefits of justice or virtue are not felt immediately. In many cases it takes a great deal of reflection, multiple experiences, and difficult attention before one can see and learn from such actions. Many, for a variety of reasons, never get to the place where they can correctly assess the value of their actions.

A necessary consequence of these truths is that the system of fatalism, in spite of the fact that many believe it to be the case, does not encourage us to commit criminal acts, or eliminate feelings of remorse. We always act according to our nature, using passions based on habits, opinions, education, and the examples that society presents to us. These things necessarily determine our conduct. So, when we are susceptible to strong passions, we are aggressive about our desires, whatever they may be. *Remorse* is the painful feeling caused by grief that is either an immediate or anticipated effect of giving in to one's passions. If these effects were always useful, we would not experience remorse, but as soon as our passions make us hated, shameful, or fearful of some form of punishment, we become restless and unhappy. We reprimand ourselves for our conduct, feeling ashamed and fearing the judgment of people that we like and who we feel like us. Our experiences teach us that the wicked person is looked down on by all who are affected by that individual's action. If the actions are not observed immediately, we know that eventually they will come to light. The slightest reflection convinces us that all wicked people are ashamed of their actions and they find themselves envious of good individuals. We are not able to enjoy the fruits of our passions without a sense of regret. Then we are ashamed and hate ourselves as our conscience torments us. Remorse follows. The truth of this is seen in the extreme precautions taken by tyrants and criminals to avoid exposure. They frequently go to great lengths to avoid public scorn. Are such people aware of their own inequities? Do they know that they are hated and contemptible? Do they feel remorse? Are they happy? Most people acquire the positive sentiments as a result of a good education. They are either strengthened or weakened by public opinion, habit, and the examples set before them. In a depraved society, remorse either does not exist or it disappears, because of the value placed on judgment by peers and leaders. There is never a feeling of shame or remorse for actions that are approved of, and practice by the majority. In corrupt governments evil people are not ashamed of their harmful actions when they are approved of by example. In immoral nations no one blushes at adultery except the spouse, at whose expense it is committed. In superstitious countries a person has no problem with murdering those with different opinions. It is clear that remorse, as well as our ideas regarding right, wrong, decency, virtue, justice, etc. are the necessary consequence of our temperament, modified by the society in which we live. Assassins and thieves, when living together, have neither shame nor remorse.

So, I repeat, all of our actions are necessary. The actions that contribute to the permanent happiness of the human species are called *virtues* and are necessarily pleasing to all who experience them, except for those whose passions and false opinions don't allow the enjoyment of the nature of things. Each of us acts and judges, necessarily, according to the ideas we have formed, be they true or false, about our happiness. There are necessary actions which we must approve of, as well as those which, despite us, we are compelled to dislike. The virtuous person and the wicked individual act from motives that are equally necessary, differing only in their perceptions about happiness. We love one out of necessity and we detest another out of the same necessity. The law of our nature, which drives us to will toward our self-preservation, does not give us the right to choose, or the free agency to prefer pain to pleasure, or vice to utility, or crime to virtue. It is our essence that forces us to discriminate between actions that are advantageous and those that go against our interests and happiness. This distinction exists even in the most corrupt societies, where the idea of virtue, although completely eroded from their conduct, remains the same in the mind. Let's suppose a person chooses a life of crime and justifies it by thinking, "Why be good in a society that is depraved and a community that is evil?" Let's also suppose that this individual has had the good fortune to escape punishment over a long series of years. I say that despite all these circumstances and good luck over the years, this person is neither happy nor content. He lives in agony, at war with his own actions and in a state of constant anxiety. How much pain and stress has he endured in this constant state of conflict with himself? How many safety measures, excessive labors, and periods of endless solitude has he endured to continue his struggle? He lives in constant fear of being found out by the community or the vengeance of his victims. Ask him what he thinks of himself and he will not answer. Ask him as he is dying and, if he is sane, he will admit that he has not known happiness or tranquility. A life of crime has filled him with stress and his own thoughts kept him from sleeping. His life has been a continuous scene of alarm, an uninterrupted chain of terror, and an everlasting anxiety of his mind. If he could do it all over he would prefer to live happily on bread and water than to possess the riches, reputation, and honor on the terms that he had acquired them. And if this criminal finds his life so dreadful how must those villains feel who have not had the same resources or advantages?

So, the system of necessity is a truth based on firm experience that establishes morals on a solid foundation. Instead of weakening the foundations of virtue, it points out its necessity, showing the constant, necessary, and strong opinions that are essential to our existence. All the prejudices and vices of our institutions, and all the effects of evil examples, have never been able to erase the foundations of virtue from our mind. When we misuse the advantages of virtue it should be blamed on the errors we have learned and the irrationality of our institutions. All our mistakes are the fatal consequences of error, the necessary result of prejudices that were part of our existence. So, let's stop saying that it's our nature to be wicked, but instead look to the harmful opinions we have been exposed to since infancy, that made us ambitious, greedy, envious, arrogant, corrupt, intolerant, obstinate, prejudiced, annoying, and mischievous. Our education plants the seeds of those vices that necessarily torment us for the rest of our lives.

Fatalism is said to discourage us by making us apathetic and destroying the bonds that should connect us with society. Its opponents say, "If everything is necessary, we must let things go on, and not be disturbed by anything." But does this *fatalism* depend on our being sensible or not? Are we the master of feeling or not feeling pain? If Nature has endowed us with a sense of humanity, is it possible that we should take a lively interest in the welfare of beings that we know are essential to our happiness? Our feelings are necessary and they depend on our specific nature which is cultivated by our education. Our imagination, which tends to concern itself with the happiness of our race, causes our hearts to be burdened by the evils we see our fellow-creatures obliged to endure. Our soul trembles when contemplating the misery that comes from the tyranny that crushes us, the superstition that leads us astray, and the passions that put us in a state of constant warfare against our neighbors. Although we know that death is the necessary end of all beings, we are still deeply saddened by the loss of a relative or a friend. Although we know a fire must burn, we always believe that we can control and stop its progress. We intimately believe that the evils to which we are a witness are the necessary consequences of primitive errors that are passed from generation to generation. If Nature has given us the necessary courage, we ought to try and speak truth to those errors. We must believe that in doing so, we will, by degrees, implement a cure for our suffering and produce the necessary changes. And if our speculations change our conduct and temperament, then we should believe that the system of necessity can have a most advantageous influence over us. Not only will it bring inner peace, but it will inspire us with a useful submission, a rational resignation, to our own destiny, by which our sensibilities frequently cause us to be overwhelmed. This happy apathy is preferable to a life filled with fear of the unknown and irrational behaviors. It would be most advantageous to the conduct and happiness of the human race, if the doctrine of fatalism resulted in the understanding that *all is necessary*. As a consequence of adopting this principle, the fatalist, if a sensible soul, would try to understand the biases of fellow-beings, and would gently try to show others the right path without ever being irritating or insulting. Indeed, what right do we have to hate or despise others because of their opinions? Aren't ignorance, vices, opinions, passions, and weaknesses the inevitable consequence of vicious institutions? Aren't most people punished enough by the multitude of evils that are troubling in so many ways? The powerful, who frequently try to crush *we the people* with an iron fist, are themselves continual victims of their own restlessness, tied to their perpetual weakness and eternal slaves to their suspicions. Is there one wicked individual who enjoys a pure, authentic, and real happiness? Do nations suffer endlessly as a result of their foolishness? Are they the continuous victims of their preconceptions? Is the ignorance of leaders, their hatred for reason and truth, reflected back to them by the stupidity of the citizens and the ruination of the states they govern? The fatalist would sadly watch necessity in action at each moment, exacting its painful verdicts on mortals who are ignorant of its power, or who feel its rebuke without being willing to acknowledge the hand that creates it. We will think that ignorance is necessary and that gullibility is the necessary result of ignorance. It will follow that slavery and bondage are the necessary consequence of ignorant gullibility, with corruption of manners coming necessarily from slavery. Finally, the miseries of society and the unhappiness of its members are the necessary offspring of this corruption. As a consequence of these ideas the fatalist will not be a sad cynic or a dangerous citizen. We will forgive our brethren who have gone astray, understanding that their errors are the necessary result of a thousand causes. We will offer them consolation and will try to inspire them with courage. We will diligently work to inform them about useful concepts, and expose the deception of idle notions and fanciful ideas. We will never display bitterness or malicious animosity toward them because that would be more likely to make them revolt from our doctrines than attract them to reason. We will not mount an insurrection against our leaders. On the contrary, we will see the necessity of their actions, even when it is to corrupt the public in order to profit from their ignorance. What we see are the inevitable effect of profound ignorance about the true interests of humans, and how everything works to keep them down.

We, the fatalist, have no right to be vain about our talents or proud of our virtues. We know that these qualities are just the consequence of our natural organization, modified by circumstances that were independent of us. We will not have hatred, or feel contempt for those whom Nature and circumstance have not favored in a similar manner. It is the fatalist who should be humble and modest as a matter of principle. Indeed, we must admit that we possess nothing that we have not previously received from an outside source. In fact, shouldn't everything lead the fatalist, whom experience has convinced of the necessity of things, to tolerance? We will see with pain that it is the essence of a society that is poorly formed, unwisely governed, enslaved to prejudice, attached to unreasonable customs, submitted to irrational laws, ruined under repression, corrupted by luxury, and drunk with false opinions. Sadly, most societies today are filled with insignificant members, composed of vicious citizens, and made up of cringing slaves who are proud of their chains. Such societies are ruled by ambitious individuals who have no idea of true glory, as well as misers, spendthrifts, and fanatics! Convinced of the necessary connection of things, the fatalist will not be surprised to see that the indifference of the leaders results in discouragement within the country, or that the influences of the powerful stir up bloody wars which are paid for with lives and resources leaving the country impoverished. We will see that the combination of these excesses is why so many nations contain individuals who want happiness but don't know how to attain it, and who are devoid of morals and virtue. In all this we will contemplate nothing more than the necessary action re-action of physics on morals and morals on physics. All who acknowledge fatality will believe that a badly governed nation is like soil that is covered with venomous reptiles and filled with poisonous plants. At some point their growth is so rampant that they began to crowd each other and choke themselves. A country cultivated by the hands of a virtuous leader will see the production of valiant citizens, of noble-minded individuals, and people with values and morals. A country cultivated by a vicious leader will find nothing but evil people with depraved hearts and contemptible souls. It is the soil, the circumstances in which we find ourselves, that makes us useful objects or prejudicial beings. The wise individual avoids one and attaches to the other. We see the wicked without anger and cherish the good with pleasure. A tree that is planted in infertile soil and a climate that stifles its growth will not produce useful fruit or shade, unlike a tree that has the fostering care of a skillful cultivator. Some will say that we degrade, undervalue and abuse humans by comparing them to a tree. Such language is used by those who are ignorant of what constitutes true dignity. A tree is an object that, when serving its purpose, combines the useful with the agreeable. It deserves our admiration when it produces sweet fruit and provides useful shade. All machines are precious when they are truly useful and faithfully perform the functions for which they are designed. Yes, I say it with courage and restate it with pleasure, the honest person, with talents and virtue is, for beings of our species, a tree that provides them with delicious fruit and refreshing shelter. The honest individual is a machine that fulfills its function when successfully meeting the expectations of all fellow beings. No, I should not blush or feel degraded to be a machine of this sort. Indeed, my heart would jump with joy if I could foresee that the fruits of my labors would one day be useful to my race and consoling to my fellow-humans. And isn't Nature herself a vast machine, of which the human species is a small and insignificant part. I see nothing shameful either in her or her productions. All the beings that come out of her are good, noble, and sublime whenever they co-operate to the production of others, and contribute to the maintenance of harmony in the sphere where they exist. Whatever the nature of the soul, be it mortal or immortal, spirit or flesh and blood, it will be viewed as noble, great, good, and sublime when associated with good individuals. It will be viewed as horrible, wicked, and corrupt when associated with men like Stalin and Hitler. Its energies will be admired and we'll be delighted and fascinated by it in a Shakespeare, in an Einstein, in a Sagan and in a Thierry. Its corruptness will be mourned when we see mean, contemptible people who praise oppression, or who submissively cringe at the foot of superstition.

All that has been said in the course of this work proves clearly that everything is necessary and always in order, relative to Nature. All beings do nothing more than follow the laws that are imposed on their respective classes. It is part of her plan that certain parts of the earth will produce delicious fruits and beautiful flowers, while others will be barren producing only poisonous vegetation. In a similar manner she has created some societies that produce wise beings and great heroes, while others only give birth to miserable souls and contemptible beings, without energy and devoid of virtue. Passions, winds, gales, hurricanes, volcanoes, wars, plagues, famines, diseases, and death are as necessary to her eternal march as are the benefits of the heat of the sun, the serenity of the atmosphere, the gentle showers of spring, plentiful years, peace, health, harmony, and life. Vice and virtue, darkness and light, and religion and science are equally necessary. One is not a benefit, and the other is not an evil, except for when they influence the happiness of beings by favoring or upsetting their particular mode of existence. *The whole cannot be miserable, but it may contain unhappy individuals.*

Nature, then, equally distributes *order* and *disorder*, *pleasure* and *pain*. By the necessity of her existence she spreads good and evil in the world in which we live. Therefore, we must not misuse her bounty or accuse her of malice. We must understand that our feeble cries and weak prayers can never arrest her colossal power, which always acts according to immutable laws. We should submit silently to our condition, and when we suffer we should not ask for help from spirits that are the creations of our misguided imaginations. Instead we must learn from Nature the remedies which she offers for the evil she creates. When she sends us diseases we must search in her bosom for those beneficial productions she has created that will cure them. When she gives us errors, she also gives us the experience to counteract them, and in truth, she gives us an antidote suitable to destroy their fatal effects. If she allows us to suffer under the pressure of vices and follies, she also shows us in virtue, a remedy for our weaknesses. If the evils that some societies experience are necessary, when those evils become unbearable the society will be forced to find remedies which Nature will always point out. And if Nature makes life unsupportable for some unfortunate beings, which she appears to have selected as her victims, death will surely deliver them from their misfortunes, although they will incorrectly be labeled as incurable. So, we should not accuse Nature of being inflexible, since for every evil she creates she also supplies a remedy for those who have the courage to find it, and the fortitude to apply it. Nature follows general and necessary laws in all her operations. Physical disaster and moral evil are not to be blamed for her lack of kindness, but to the necessity of things. Physical disaster is the imbalance produced in our organs by physical causes that we see and experience. Moral evil is the imbalance produced in us by physical causes of which we are not aware. These causes always end by creating effects that strike the senses. Neither thought nor the will to act come into play until they receive impulses that result from the aforementioned causes. We suffer because some beings survive at the expense of the body. We enjoy because some beings are in sync with their mode of existence. We are born because it's the nature of some form of matter to combine with a determinate form. We live, act, and think because it is the essence of certain combinations to live by given means for a season. We die because a necessary law insists that all the combinations which are formed shall either be destroyed or dissolved. From all this we can see that Nature is impartial to all its productions. She submits us, like all other beings, to those eternal laws from which she has not even exempted herself. If she was to suspend these laws, even for an instant, from that moment disorder would reign in her system. Her harmony would be disturbed.

Those who want to study Nature must use experience as a guide. This and only this will allow them to dive into her secrets, to discover by degrees the frequently unrevealed cry of those slender causes, from which we are able to operate the greatest phenomena. Via the aid of experience, we frequently discover properties and modes of action that were entirely unknown to those who came before us. In many cases, effects that were thought to be marvelous or supernatural have become simple and natural consequences of causes that we understand and can explain. As a result of probing Nature, we understand the causes of earthquakes, hurricanes, tsunamis, meteors, tornados, lightening, etc. all of which were considered by our ancestors, and still are by some, as unquestionable signs of heavens wrath. Future generations, in following up, in studying the experiences already documented, will perhaps go further and discover causes that are currently unknown. The united efforts of the human species will perhaps someday shed light on the mysteries of Nature that she has refused to divulge to all researchers.

In thinking about us and our true characteristics, we will cast aside authority to follow experience and avoid error by consulting reason. When we submit everything to physical laws, which our imagination has exerted its utmost power to ignore, we will find that the moral world follows the exact same rules as those of the physical world. Most of the astonishing effects, which ignorance aided by biases make us think of as unexplainable and wonderful, are natural consequences flowing from simple causes. We will find that the eruption of a volcano and the birth of a conqueror are to Nature the same thing. Think back to the primitive causes of the striking events that were viewed with fearful alarm. The sources of the terrible revolutions, frightful tremors, and dreadful explosions that destroyed nations and tore up societies by their roots were moved by physical causes, wills that brought about the most surprising and extensive changes, were so inconsequential that we completely ignore them. We believed these causes utterly incapable of giving birth to events that strike us with awe and fill us with so much amazement. So, if we were to judge causes by their effects, there would be no small causes in the universe. In Nature where everything is connected, where everything acts and reacts, moves and changes, composes and decomposes, forms and destroys, there is not an atom which does not play an important part. Every particle, no matter how minute, when placed in the right circumstances, creates the most extraordinary effects. If we could follow the eternal chain of events that connect all causes with the effects we witness, that is, if we could unravel the threads that give impulse to thought, decision to the will, and direction to passions of individuals who are called mighty, we would find that Nature uses atoms to move the moral world. It is the unexpected but necessary function of these minute particles of matter, via their combinations and proportions, to change us by degrees without our knowledge; all making us think, will, and act in a determinate but necessary manner. If the will and actions of an individual have an influence over a great number of other people, the result is the moral world in a state of combustion, and the ensuing consequences are contemplated with fearful wonder. Too much bitterness in the heart of a fanatic, too much passion in the heart of a conqueror, a painful indigestion in the stomach of a king, a whim that passes in the mind of a woman, are sometimes sufficient causes to: go to war; send millions to be slaughtered; genocide; reduce cities to ashes; plunge nations into slavery; put a nation in mourning; breed famine; bring about an epidemic; propagate calamity; extend misery; or spread desolation far and wide upon the surface of our planet over a long series of ages.

The dominant passions of an individual of the human species can override the passions of others, while uniting and influencing the wills of many, to decide the human condition. This is how an ambitious, crafty, and voluptuous Arab influenced his countrymen with the effect being the subjugation and desolation of vast countries in Asia, Africa, and Europe. The consequences were strong enough to form a new, extensive, and slavish empire. It gave a new religion to millions of human beings causing them to give up their former Gods. He altered opinions and changed the customs of a considerable portion of the population of earth. But in examining the primitive sources of this strange revolution, what were the hidden causes that influenced this man? What excited his unique passions and modified his temperament? What combinations of matter resulted in such a crafty, ambitious, enthusiastic, and eloquent man? How did this person, who was able to make his fellow being concur to his extravagant views, come to be? He was born, nourished, and raised like any other yet there were thousands of transitory causes that made him a passionate and important being with the ability to change the face of this mundane sphere. Yet the slightest change in any one of those causes would have stopped or changed the entire movement. A different diet, a glass of water, a drop of blood, might have been enough to save kingdoms. So, the condition of the human species, as well as that of each individual, depends at every instant on unconscious causes that unrelated circumstances, opportunities, and convenience put into action. We attribute their effects to chance, but in reality, these causes operate necessarily and act according to fixed rules. We do not have the wisdom or the honesty to go back to their true principles, regarding such feeble motives with contempt because we have been taught to believe that they cannot create such amazing effects. These motives, weak as they appear to be, apply the necessary laws that are sufficient in the hands of Nature to move the universe. So we see that the unknown causes, concealed in the bosom of Nature, frequently decide our fate the moment their action is displayed. The happiness or sorrow and the prosperity or misery of each individual, as well as that of nations, are caused by powers that are impossible to foresee, understand, or control. Perhaps at this moment atoms are combining to form unknown particles to create a leader who will be the curse or the savior of a mighty nation. We do not determine our destiny for one single instant. We are not aware of the causes acting inside the body, nor are we aware of the circumstances that will move them to action. Our condition in life is determined by causes that we cannot figure out and that are not known to us. Frequently an unforeseen encounter, either passive or aggressive, results in a passion that will have an influence over one's happiness. It is in this way that a virtuous individual, by whimsical combination of unanticipated circumstances, may become in an instant the most criminal of the species. Although this truth appears to be frightful and terrible, isn't it more valuable to know that an infinity of occurrences that we have no control over can, at every instant, take away the life to which we are so strongly attached? Fatalism makes it easier for a good person to face death. In a society filled with evil, it is a way to withdraw from the wickedness. Death is viewed as a medium between life and the misfortunes that destroy happiness.

You should submit to necessity, because despite yourself, it will always hurry you forward. Resign to Nature, accepting the good she presents, and opposing the necessary evil she makes you experience by looking to her for solutions. Do not allow your mind to be filled with useless thoughts. Learn to enjoy moderation because pain is the necessary companion of excess. Follow the path of virtue because everything will prove, even in this irrational world, that it is absolutely necessary to make you honorable in the eyes of others and content with yourself.

Feeble, vain mortal, you pretend to be a free agent. Alas, don't you see all the threads that enchain you? Don't you know that you are made of atoms, and it is them that move you? They are the circumstances independent of yourself that modify your being, over which you have no control, and that determine your destiny? Under the powerful influence of Nature that controls you, will you pretend to be the only being capable of resisting her power? Do you really think that your weak prayers will persuade her to stop her eternal march, and that your sickly desires can force her to change her everlasting course?

Chapter 13

The Immortality of the Soul; The Doctrine of a Future State; The Fear of Death

The reflections presented to the reader in this work tend to show what should be thought of the human soul, as well as what it is made of and how it works. Everything proves, in a most convincing manner, that it acts and moves, like all other beings, according to the laws of Nature, and cannot be distinguished from the body. It is born with the body and grows up with it. It is modified in the same ways and it perishes with the body in death. The soul experiences infancy, at which time it stores infinitely many ideas which it receives from exterior objects through its organs. In this way it collects information and experiences that, whether true or false, result in the formation of a system of conduct which cause it to act and think in a certain manner. From this comes its happiness or its misery, its reason or its disorientation, and its vices or its virtues. When it and the body reach full maturity it does not stop for an instant experiencing sensations, be they agreeable or disagreeable. It shares all the pleasures and pains, and conjointly approves or disapproves of its state. It is always healthy or sick, active or inactive, and awake or asleep. When a person grows old and loses the ability to think clearly as well as sight, hearing, flexibility, imagination, and reflexes, what happens to the soul? Alas, it sinks down with the body losing feeling and becoming sluggish as decay overtakes activity. It suffers the pains the body feels as the years take their toll. This substance which is deemed spiritual, immaterial, and distinguished from matter, undergoes all the modifications the body experiences. In spite of this proof that the soul is material and connected with the body, so convincing to the open minded, there are some who feel that, although the body perishes, the soul does not. They believe that this part of a human being enjoys the special privilege of *immortality*, making it exempt from dissolution and free from the changes that all beings in Nature undergo. Consequently, some have convinced themselves that this privileged soul does not die. Its immortality, above all, is undeniable to those who think of it as spiritual. After making it a simple being without extent and devoid of parts, which is totally different than anything we have ever seen, we pretend that it is not subject to the laws of decomposition, which is common to all beings and which experience shows us continuously.

Upon feeling the hidden forces that produce action and give direction to the motions of the body, and being ignorant of and unacquainted with the energies of Nature, some decided that the same forces that move the soul and the body must move Nature. So, after deciding that humans consist of two parts, it was concluded that Nature must be the same. Separating Nature from her source of energy, by degrees she was made spiritual. This is how Nature became thought of as the soul of the world. The soul of human beings is thought to be derived from this universal soul. It was believed that *God formed man from dust and breathed into his nostrils the breath of life; and man became a living soul.* Today's Catholics reject this system of divine creation since it supposes the soul is part of the Divinity, making Him divisible, which would be inconvenient to the Roman Catholic idea of purgatory or the system of everlasting punishment. Subsequent religions have renounced these advantages which they judge as incompatible with other parts of their systems. They rejected that the ruler of Nature or her maker was the soul of humans. Instead, in His omnipotence, He created a human soul for each body. These souls then animated the body with life and, because of the same omnipotence, enjoyed immortality. The bottom line is that those who believe the soul is part of the Divinity think that after the death of the body, which serves as an envelope for the soul, it returns to its original source. Those who do not adopt the idea of the soul being part of the Divinity, do admire the spirituality and believe in the immortality of the soul. As such, they had to imagine a place for these souls to reside after the death of the body. Their imaginations painted residences based on their greatest hopes, desires, fears, and prejudices.

Nothing is more popular than the doctrine of the *immortality of the soul*, and nothing is more universally taught than the expectation of another life. Nature has instilled in us the strongest love for our existence, so the desire to preserve ourselves forever was a necessary consequence. This desire was converted to certainty when we made arguments to prove that we would never cease to exist. Whatever the origins, we listened with great interest to those who announced a system so in sync with our wishes. Some espoused that our soul has no useless desires and that it desires eternal life. Then, by a very strange logic, not uncommon to the formation of religious beliefs, it was concluded that this desire could not fail to be fulfilled. The more logical among us recognized the immortality of the soul to be an innate idea in humans. Regardless of all of this, we should not be surprised about our desire to exist forever, which always was and will be part of our essence. The fact that we received with eagerness a hypothesis that flattered our hopes, by promising that our desires would one day be fulfilled, should come as no revelation. But is the desire for immortality, which occupies so much of our thinking, unquestionable proof of the reality of this future life? Our passion for existence is a natural consequence of the tendency of a sensible being to want to conserve oneself. In human beings the energy of the soul, which keeps pace with the imagination, always recognizes that which is strongly desired. And just as we desire life of the body and are frustrated, isn't the soul's desire for life also frustrated? Those who believe in immortality argue, "All people desire to live forever, therefore all people will live forever." They feel this is a valid argument and expect it to be accepted by all. But, if it was asserted, "All people naturally desire to be rich, therefore all people will one day be rich," how many believers would this doctrine find?

The simplest reflection on the nature of the soul should convince us that the idea of its immortality is only an illusion of the brain. Indeed what is the soul if it is not the senses? To think, to enjoy, and to suffer is to feel. Life is a combination of all the changes and motions that organized beings experience. So when a body dies its sensibilities stop functioning. It is no longer capable of having ideas and consequently thoughts. We've proven that ideas can only reach us through our senses. Yet they want us to believe that even though we are deprived of our senses we are still able to receive ideas, have perceptions, and form ideas. The soul that they've created is a being separate from the human body. Life in a body is the totality of its motions. Feelings and thoughts are part of this motion, so it's reasonable to suppose that in a dead person these motions will cease, like all others. What reasoning can be used to prove that this soul, which feels, thinks, wills, and acts via the aid of our organs, can experience any feelings whatsoever when the organs are dead? Isn't it evident that the soul depends on the different body parts and the order in which they perform their functions, which is the combined motion of the whole? So, when the body is destroyed doesn't it make sense to conclude that the soul will be destroyed also? Don't we see that during the course of human life the soul is stimulated, changed, deranged, and disturbed by all the changes our organs experience? Yet it is insisted that this soul acts, thinks, and exists when these same organs have entirely disappeared!

An organized being could be compared to a clock, which once broken is no longer suitable for telling time. To say the soul can feel, think, enjoy, and suffer after the body is dead is like saying that a clock that has been smashed into a thousand pieces will continue to tell time. Those who say that the soul can exist after the body is dead must support the completely absurd idea that the body can conserve itself after its destruction. Believers will say that the conservation of the soul after death is an act of Divine Omnipotence. But this is supporting an absurdity with a meaningless hypothesis. It surely doesn't mean by Divine Omnipotence, whatever that is, that a thing will exist and not exist at the same time. Unless you accept this it will be difficult to prove that a soul can feel and think without the organs and senses necessary for thought.

At the very least, it must be admitted that the doctrine of the immortality of the soul and the expectation of a future life are hard concepts for a reasonable person to accept. These notions, which were formed to flatter us and disturb the imagination of uninformed individuals who are not able to reason, cannot appear to be either convincing or likely to enlightened minds. Reason, which does not allow for prejudice, is set back by the idea of a soul that feels, thinks, rejoices, becomes sick, and has ideas, all without having organs. They want you to believe that a soul destitute of the only known mediums for feeling sensations, having perceptions, and forming ideas can perform all of those functions. If one argues that *supernatural* or *unknown* means exist for transmitting ideas to the soul, separate from the body, why are these means known only to some and not all? It can be said with certainty and without controversy that the fatalist, who believes in the necessity of ideas, must reject the doctrine of the immortality of the soul, which contradicts the basic principles of fatalism.

In defiance of the peace so many say will come with eternal existence and despite the firm belief so many have that the soul will survive the body, many seem alarmed about the dissolution of the body. They don't want to think about their death, which they should desire as the end of so many miseries, but instead anticipate with great restlessness. It is so true that the real, the present, even with its trials and hardships, has much more influence over mankind than the most beautiful imaginings of a life after death, which can only be viewed through clouds of uncertainty. Even the most religious individuals, in spite of expressing a conviction about a blessed eternity, don't find these exaggerated hopes sufficient to repress fears and prevent trembling when considering the necessary dissolution of the body. For humans, death has always been feared and viewed as a strange occurrence, contrary to the order of things and opposed to Nature. It is viewed as an effect of celestial vengeance or as the *wages of sin*. Although everything proves that death is inevitable, we are never able to truly accept the idea and rarely think about it without shuddering. So, the assurance of possessing an immortal soul is a feeble consolation for the grief we feel about our perishable body. Regarding death, two causes strengthen our fears and feed our alarm. One is that death, frequently accompanied by pain, takes us from an existence that we are used to and that pleases us. The second is the uncertainty of the state that must succeed our actual existence. Men fear death for the same reasons that children fear being alone in the dark. We naturally challenge everything to which we are not acquainted. We want to clearly see so that we can avoid harm and move toward desirable objects. As a living being, we cannot form any idea of non-existence, since this idea disturbs us due to our lack of experience. At this point the imagination goes to work and creates good or bad views of this uncertain state. Being used to thinking, feeling, and enjoying, which in our present state are so necessary, we view anything that will deprive us of these sensations, as well as being plunged into nothingness, as undesirable to say the least. And even if death is painless, we always look at it as a troubling loneliness and a heap of profound darkness. We see it as a state of desolation, without help, and we feel the permanence of this frightful situation very deeply. But shouldn't a sound sleep, when we are aware of nothing, give us a true idea of this state. Is death anything more than a profound and permanent sleep? Isn't this idea better than forming an idea that makes us dread death? If we could form a true image of this state, we would no longer fear it. But since we cannot conceive a state without feelings, we believe that after death we will still have the same feelings and consciousness of things which, in the mind, are frequently sad and gloomy. We imagine our funeral and the things people will say about us. We convince ourselves that these events will affect us with as much emotion as they would if we were still in possession of our senses.

Mortals, misled by fear! After you die your eyes will no longer see, your ears will no longer hear, and from the depth of your grave you will not be a witness to the world of which you were a part. To die is to stop thinking, feeling, enjoying, and suffering. Your ideas will perish with you and your sorrows will not follow you to your silent tomb. Don't think of death with fear or sadness, but with peace and happiness, knowing that the terrors so many labored to instill in you are false. The fears of death are vain illusions that must disappear as soon we learn to view this necessary event with truth. Philosophy has been defined as *a meditation on death*. We are not saying that we should preoccupy our thoughts with fear and sorrow about our end. On the contrary, we are saying to understand it as something Nature requires of all its beings, and to expect it with a serene perspective. If life is a gift and it's necessary to love it, it is no less necessary to quit it. Reason should teach us all to accept the decrees of fate with calm resignation. Our welfare insists that we form the habit of contemplating with calmness, not alarm, an event that our essence makes inevitable. Our interest demands that we should not clutch sadly to our perceived misfortune and let continual dread embitter our lives. How can one enjoy the pleasures life offers if we are continually looking to its end with fear? Reason and interests should work together to stifle the vague terrors that the imagination inspires. They are the best tools to think about an object we have no knowledge of other than the hideous superstitious ideas to which we were exposed. We must work to rid death of these vain illusions and think of it as the sleep of a lifetime. Indeed, it is a sleep that will have no bad dreams and from which an unpleasant awakening is never likely to follow. To die is to sleep, that is to enter a state of insensibility that we were in prior to birth, when we had no senses and were not conscious of our actual existence. Laws, as necessary as those which resulted in birth, will make us return to the bosom of Nature. After death we will be reproduced under some new form which would be useless for us to know. Without consulting us, Nature places each of us for a season in the order of organized beings. Without our consent, she will oblige us to quit it to occupy some other order. And we should not complain that Nature is cruel. She only holds us to a law from which no one of her beings is exempt. Some complain about the short duration of life and how time flies, yet most don't know how to employ time or enjoy life. If all are born and perish, and if everything is changed and destroyed, why should humans, with our frail bodies, be exempt from the common law that says even the earth must undergo changes and will someday be destroyed. Feeble, frail mortal! You pretend to exist forever. So, for you alone Nature will change her undeviating course? Don't you see comets and planets that are subject to death? Live in peace for the season that Nature gives you. If your mind is enlightened by reason you will die without terror!

In spite of the simplicity of these reflections it is rare indeed to find individuals who truly are not afraid of death. The wise person turns pale as it approaches unless the mind has been prepared to expect it with serenity. It should come as no surprise that the idea of death is so revolting to the average person. It scares the young, it doubles the resolve of the middle aged, and it even adds to the sorrow of the old, who are worn down by life and its trials. Indeed, the old frequently dread it much more than the young, who are full of life's energy. The individual who has lived many years becomes more attached to existence with each passing year. None the less, the powers of the mind weaken as labors, sickness, and pain take their toll on the body and the mind. The will becomes faint and superstitious terrors seem more frightening. Eventually we are consumed by disease, sometimes accompanied by excruciating pain that tortures the individual. Even this unhappy person, who has been plunged into misfortune, rarely dares to contemplate death, which should be viewed as an end to the suffering. And if the source of this fear were to be identified, it would be found in our nature, which attaches us to life. It is a deficiency of energy in the soul that everything works to break down, and superstition, which instead of strengthening, contributes to the weakness. To make it worse, nearly all human institutions, and the opinions of many people, conspire to strengthen our fears making ideas of death all the more terrible and revolting. Superstition alone takes pride in presenting death as a most frightful experience. It paints death with the most disgusting colors, making it a dreadful moment which not only puts an end to our pleasures, but gives us up, without defense, to a strange trial which will end with a merciless judgment, which nothing can soften. According to this superstition, the most virtuous individual has reason to fear, knowing the most dreadful torments and endless punishment await the victims to involuntary weakness. Every person must pay for the necessary faults of a short life, including our weaknesses, momentary offenses, the tendencies that were planted in our hearts, the errors of the mind, and the opinions that we learned. We bear the burden of the society we were born into without our consent, the ideas we formed, the passions we indulged to excess, and not being able to understand all that religions offered us. Our shortcomings in any of these areas are avenged with the most severe and never-ending penalties. Ixion is tied to his wheel forever. Sisyphus must roll his stone for all of eternity without ever reaching the top of his mountain. Prometheus will watch the vulture eat his liver for all of perpetuity. All who refuse to listen to the spiritual leaders, or pay homage to their Gods, or dare to consult reason, or boldly look to expose impostors, are sentenced to an eternity of the most excruciating agonies in a sea of liquid brimstone, wailing and gnashing their teeth! Is it any wonder that we fear death?

This is how superstition affects its unhappy and gullible believers. These are the fears that the tyrants of human thought point out as truth. Many accept the notion of a God to avoid these eternal outcomes. Even those who are converted or "born again" can be viewed as the most convincing argument for the abnormalities of our species. None the less, it will be shown that these systems, or rather these superstitious beliefs, so terrible to think about, have little effect on most of mankind. Most mortals rarely think about superstitious consequences, and completely ignore them in moments when passion, interest, pleasure, or example, hurry us along. These fears usually act on good people, making honest hearts tremble, but have no effect on the evil. They torment sensible souls and gentle minds, but have no effect on those rebellious spirits who are set in their ways. They alarm none but those who are already sufficiently alarmed, coercing only those who are already restrained. These notions impress nothing on the wicked except to double the wickedness of their natural character, justifying it in their own eyes, and giving them excuses to follow it without fear or hesitation. Indeed, experience over the years has shown the excessive wickedness that passions have led some into, frequently with the authorization of the church, including, but not limited to, the abuse of children by priests, the approval to kill Jews, the burning of non-believers at the stake, etc. The perpetrators of such acts are frequently unchained by superstition, or at least able to justify their action as religious acts. People have never been more ambitious, jealous, crafty, cruel, and vicious than when convinced that superstition permits or commands such actions. Superstition did nothing more than lend an invincible force to natural passions, allowing some to exercise them with freedom and without remorse, all with the blessings of the church. As such, the most evil of acts were performed by the most evil of individuals who believed that by displaying an over-heated zeal, they were earning the right to a place in heaven.

These effects which are produced on mortals are the *beneficial* concepts of superstition. These reflections provide an answer to those who say, "If heaven is promised equally to the wicked as well as the righteous, no one would believe in another life." We reply that in fact heaven frequently is a home to the most useless and depraved of our species. Would a list of saints in heaven consist of nothing but righteous and good people? And don't some religions say that women will never be allowed into heaven? Heaven is said to be a place for only the virtuous, yet the person who tortures some unfortunate wretch whose only crime is believing in a different God, expects to be rewarded for this deed with everlasting happiness. Aren't many promised eternal salvation for their belief in the right God? Are humans, mistake ridden and feeble, with all their faults, competent to make judgments about the heavenly rewards of fellow beings? With our limited vision can we gauge the depths of the human heart in such a way that we can determine with sufficient precision who among us is gifted enough to earn a blessed eternity? This is how wicked people are held up as models by superstition, which as we will see, sharpens the passions of those disposed to evil, by legitimizing crimes that would normally be viewed as acts of terror. The priests of superstition give the most reckless followers the power to give in to their angry passions, and instead of feeling fear or shame or being prosecuted, they are promised eternal happiness.

With respect to the unbelievers, there are no doubt wicked individuals among them, as well as among believers, but being an unbeliever no more implies wickedness then believing implies righteousness. On the contrary, the person who thinks and contemplates is more likely on a true path to goodness than the follower who is blindly guided by uncertain motives or the interests of others. Sensible people have the greatest advantage when examining opinions that they are told will have an influence over their eternal happiness. If such opinions are found to be false, or appear to be harmful, sensible people will be able to decide that there is no need to fear or to hope for another life. They will be able to avoid vices that would result in injury to themselves and the contempt of their neighbors and society. The person who does not expect another life is more interested in living this life as long and as well as possible, cultivating virtue, endearing fellow beings, and performing the duties of the only life we have any knowledge of with discipline. Sensible people have made great strides toward happiness, while disengaging from the terrors that afflict others, which frequently prevents them from acting. Such individuals have nothing to fear and everything to hope for over the course of a life. And if, contrary to our judgment, there is a hereafter existence, were our actions regulated by virtue, and did we do all we could to contribute to the happiness of ourselves and our species?

Superstition, in fact, takes pride in making us lazy. It molds us into believers and makes us fearful. Its main purpose is to constantly worry us, reminding us of the horrors of death, and tormenting us not only in this life but beyond. In order to keep their followers, its priests invented future regions with a variety of heavenly rewards and hellish punishments, which only they had the power to dispense based on one's ability to effortlessly yield to their arbitrary laws. Far from consoling us, cultivating reason, and teaching us to yield to necessity, superstition strives to make death a still more bitter and heavy burden, filling it with a multitude of hideous phantoms, painting it with frightful colors, and making its approach terrible. This is how the world has become filled with either enthusiasts who are seduced by vague promises, or shameful slaves who are coerced with fears of imaginary evils. It has convinced us that life is only a journey to a more important life. This doctrine, whether rational or irrational, keeps us from seeking true happiness through the improvement of our institutions and laws, progress in science, and perfecting our morals. Instead, vain and gloomy ideas absorb our attention, as we consent to groan under fanatical tyranny, squirm under political mandates, live in error, and languish in misfortune, all with the hope that after death we will be happy. We firmly believe that after death, our tragedies and our patience will conduct us to never-ending happiness. We allow ourselves to be controlled by cruel priests who make us purchase our future welfare at the expense of everything dear to our peace and most valuable to our existence here on earth. We are told that we will not be welcome in heaven and will suffer eternally if we make any effort to get away from their power. This is how the doctrine of a future life has been so detrimental to the human species. It has plunged whole nations into laziness and indifference about their present welfare, or it hurried them into the most furious enthusiasm that they ended up tearing each other to pieces in order to earn the promised heaven.

Some may ask, "How did we come up with the idea of another world?" In truth, we have no idea of a future life, so ideas from the past and present furnished the imagination with the materials to construct the places where we would spend eternity. In reality, we have two modes of feeling, one that we like, and another that we dislike. Persuaded that these two modes will always be with us, even after death, we created two eternal homes, one a place of happiness and the other a place of misery. One contains all who obey the calls of superstition, who believe in its dogmas, while the other is a prison created to avenge the cause of heaven on all who do not faithfully believe the doctrines espoused by the ministers of a wide variety of superstitions. Anyone who gives any thought to the necessary consequence of this reasoning will see that the first place is completely useless due to the number of systems and contradictions that result. No matter which one we believe and follow in a faithful manner, we must still be ranked as a rebel to the Divinity, because we cannot believe in all, and those that we do not follow condemn us to the prison-house. Such is the origin of the ideas of a future life, so different to so many. Look anywhere and you'll find a heavenly father and an evil under lord, a paradise and a hell. Two distinct places constructed according to the imagination of enthusiasts who invented them based on their own prejudices, hopes, and fears, and meant to influence the people who believe in them. The Indians made their heaven a place of permanent rest because living in a hot climate they viewed comfort as the ultimate happiness. The Muslims promised themselves physical pleasures, like those that are the object of their prayers in life.

Whatever the nature of these pleasures, we anticipated that a body was needed for our soul to be able to enjoy the pleasures or experience the pains that awaited us. From this kind of thinking came the doctrine of the *resurrection*. But, as we watched the body decay, rot, and dissolve, as we witnessed decomposition, we were at a loss for how to get back the body that was so necessary. We had no choice but to go back to the Divine Omnipotence, who has the power to restore the body. This story, so incomprehensible, has many followers who have never given it any serious examination. Of course, the doctrine of resurrection is useless to all who believe that the soul feels, thinks, suffers, and enjoys after it leaves the body. Indeed, there are sects who maintain that the body is not necessary, and as such will not be resurrected. In effect the soul has no need for a body or any exterior being in order to experience sensations or to have ideas. Others say that the rejected soul will see everything in the Divinity, feeling themselves burn, without having a body. And some, not able to elevate themselves to these sublime notions, believe that we never cease to exist after death, but take the form of different animals that inhabit the earth. This belief is referred to as the doctrine of Reincarnation.

As for hell, the imaginations of fanatics, who wanted to control people, assembled the most frightful images to make it all the more terrible. Fire, which produces a most painful sensation, was the main ingredient in the creation of hell. Not finding a crueler form of everlasting punishment for non-believers, the imaginations of the creators of hell were obliged to stop there. The priests of the various religions generally agreed that fire would one day avenge their offended divinities. As such, they preached that their angry Gods would confine all who questioned their creeds to fiery dungeons, perpetually rolling in a vortex of bituminous flames, plunged in an unfathomable sea of liquid Sulphur, making the infernal caverns echo with their useless groans and their never-ending gnashing of teeth. But it may be asked, how can we accept the belief in a God associated with eternal torments, especially when so many who preached it had reason to fear it themselves? Why would we accept such a revolting idea? First, very few people who resort to critical thinking and reason ever believe such absurdities. But for those who counterbalance their divinity with goodness and mercy, such dogma becomes acceptable. Secondly, those who are blinded with fear never think about the strangeness of such doctrines, which they receive with awe from priests, or which were transmitted to them by their fathers. Thirdly, each sees the terror of hell as distant, especially since superstition promises the means of escaping the tortures believed to be earned. Still, like sick people who cling to the most painful lives, some prefer the idea of an unhappy existence to one of no existence, which is the most frightful evil that can happen. They do so either because they cannot form any idea about it, or their imagination paints non-existence, nothingness, as the confused assemblage of all evils. A known evil, no matter how terrible, scares us less, especially if we can avoid it, than an evil of which we know nothing and that the imagination is painfully focused on, but for which we have no remedy.

We can see that *superstition*, rather than consoling us about the necessity of death, only makes it more terrible by pretending that it will be followed by the greatest of evils and miseries. What can be said about a belief so destructive to society, yet adopted by so many nations? It tells the people that at any moment they can be taken to a most rigorous judgment. The idea of a world always on the brink of dissolution is better suited to terrify, discourage, and dampen the desire of improving our condition. Imagine a divinity sitting on the ruins of Nature passing judgment on the human species. These are the ideas that minds of nations have been fed for thousands of years. They are so dangerous that if we tried to follow all of them faithfully we would fall into the most abject stupidity. How could we occupy our thinking with the idea of a perishable world that could crumble into atoms at any moment? How could we dream about making ourselves happy on earth when we must view it as the porch to an eternal kingdom? Not surprisingly, it follows that superstitions gave way to other doctrines that required total detachment from the most innocent of earthly pleasures. As a result we become lazy, indifferent, unsociable, and miserable souls, which make us useless to ourselves and dangerous to others. If necessity did not force us to put aside the practices of these irrational systems, and our wants did not bring us back to reason despite these superstitious doctrines, the world would become a vast desert inhabited by a few isolated savages. We must put these notions aside so that human associations can exist.

None the less, the doctrine of a future life, along with rewards and punishments, have been regarded for a great many ages as the most powerful, and possibly the only, motive for controlling our passions and the only way we can be forced to be virtuous. By degrees, this doctrine has become the basis of most religions and political systems to the extent that some believe that life without it would destroy the fabric of society. The founders of superstition have used it to influence their gullible disciples, while legislators see it as the best way to control the masses, and religions tell us it is necessary for our eternal happiness. Many philosophers sincerely believe that this doctrine, which terrifies us, is the only way to keep us from a life of crime. When the doctrine of the immortality of the soul was first taught it caused a large number of men who were unhappy with their lives to commit suicide. Regardless, this doctrine of superstition has been most useful when given to nations by those who made themselves its leaders. It was the foundation of their power, the source of their wealth, and the basis of the blindness that resulted in terrors that they wanted to instill in the human race. This doctrine made priest more powerful than kings. Because of this dogma, nations are filled with enthusiasts who are drunk with superstition, always more likely to listen to its dangers, or to the orders of its leaders, than to the guidance of reason, the cries of Nature, or the laws of society. Politics became a slave to the whims of religious leaders. The progressive ruler was force to bend under the weight of the rule of superstition. The first exerted power in this world, the latter extended power into the world to come, which was much more important for mortals on earth who are only a pilgrims and mere passengers. So the doctrine of another life placed governments in a state of dependence on priests and religions. The ruler is nothing more than the first subject and is never obeyed unless the two are in agreement. Nature cried out to us, in vain, to enjoy our present happiness. The priests ordered us to be unhappy now, but expect happiness after death. Reason urged us, in vain, to be peaceable. The priests taught fanaticism and ranted about fury, obliging his subjects to disturb the public peace every time there was a question about the supposed interests of the invisible ruler of another life and the real interests of these same priests.

Such are the fruits that politics gained from the doctrine of a future life. Belief in a world to come has enabled religious zealots to conquer the present world. The expectation of celestial happiness and the fear of future tortures only serve to prevent us from seeking the means to make ourselves happy here and now. So, error under any circumstances will always be a source of evil for mankind. The doctrine of another life and the idea of eternal happiness will turn mortals into enthusiastic believers. Overwhelming people with fears will make them useless beings and cowards, or furious individuals who lose sight of this life, and focus on the world to come with the dreadful evils that may accompany death.

For those who believe that the doctrine of future rewards and punishments is the most powerful way to control our passions, they only need to look at the world around them. We see this assertion contradicted everywhere we look. We see that these marvelous speculations, which cannot change our temperament, do not in any way lessen the number of wicked people, which is the result of passions fueled by the vices that societies instill. In nations that are most convinced of future punishments we see all forms of criminals who pretend they believe in the reality of an afterlife, yet in the vortex of pleasures and the fury of their passions, their belief in this formidable future existence dissipates. In those moments, the fear of future tortures has no influence over their earthly conduct. So, in countries where the doctrine of another life is so firmly established that common people defend it and become irritated with anyone who expresses doubt, they seem to ignore unjust leaders who neglect the welfare of their people or who are criminals themselves. In these societies there are an abundance of misers, extortionist, crooks, and vicious individuals, some of whom are priests. They get paid to preach about the vengeance of heaven against vices which they themselves encourage by example. If you ask them how they dare to give in to temptations that will earn them eternal punishment, they will reply that the madness of their passions, or the force of their habits, or the contagious examples, or even the power of circumstances, controlled them and made them forget about the dreadful consequences of their actions. Then they will fall back on the treasure of divine mercy, which is infinite and will forgive the foulest of acts, remove guilt, and erase the most enormous of crimes. Of the many wicked people who commit crimes against society, you will find only a small number who are sufficiently intimidated by the fears of a miserable afterlife to resist their predispositions. Basically, the threat of a hereafter is not strong enough to overcome a person's tendencies, just as the law and fear of jail are not sufficient motives to keep some from committing criminal acts. Indeed, only fearful and timid souls, who are born into the world with moderate passions, weak organization, and less active imaginations, fear the terrors of another life. Those who are already restrained by Nature find that the fear of future punishments counterbalances the weak efforts of their feeble passions. Completely different are the sinners, the hardened criminals, and the habitually vicious, whose unimaginable excesses will be stopped by nothing, and who, in their violence, shut their eyes to fear of the law in this world and despise even more those of the next. Yet, we must ask, how many people say they are, and believe themselves to be, restrained by fears of the life to come? Those who say they are deceive us and themselves by not recognizing that these fears are the result of motives like: the weakness of their machine; the mildness of their temperament; the slender energy of their souls; their natural timidity; the ideas given to them as part of their education; the fear of societal consequences of criminal actions; and the physical consequences that always follow evil actions. These are the true motives that restrain them, not the notions of a future life, which those who say they firmly believe in its existence forget when a powerful interest solicits them to sin. If we could look closely at the fears we attribute to Gods and religious dogma, we would see that some fear their own weaknesses and cowardliness and have only a small interest to commit evil. These people would act the same way with or without the fear of afterlife punishments. If we could reflect clearly, we would see that it is always necessity that makes us act as we do.

We cannot be restrained when we do not have within us the motives that are strong enough to bring us back to reason. There is nothing in this world or the next that can make us virtuous when our organization is unfavorable, the mind badly educated, the imagination violent, habits incurable, examples fatal, and powerful interests invite us at every turn to a life of crime. Nothing can stop the individual who does not care about public opinion, despises the law, can ignore the conscience, and whose position of power in this world eliminates the possibility of punishment. Through all of this persons violent actions, fear of a distant future is minimal. The idea of eternal punishment recedes before performing the necessary acts that address more immediate interests and are consistent with immediate happiness. All powerful passions blind us to everything that is not the immediate object of those passions. The terrors of a future life are easily diminished by our desires, especially in the wicked person who does not fear the much closer punishment of the law and does not care about being hated by fellow beings. When we decide to commit a crime we see no certainty except the supposed advantage of the act. The rest always appears to be false or problematic.

If we would take a moment to think, we would realize that using the punishments of an avenging Deity is not the way to stop hardened criminals who come into the world as naturally self-loving and peaceful people. The criminal will give into desires with or without religion. Those individuals who will not be moved by the threat of distant punishments cannot see the results of their evil actions. Nor can they see the hate and anger that their actions create in fellow beings. They look with resentment on the earthly punishments that must be endured. The tyrant with a cold and callous heart who causes misery and distress for an entire nation will not fear the anger of a more powerful master. And when an arrogant despot pretends to be accountable for his actions to the Divinity alone, it is because he fears his nation more than he does his God.

On the other hand, doesn't superstition itself, and even religion, destroy the effects of the fears which it professes to be beneficial? Don't they provide believers a means of freeing themselves from the punishments with which it tries to torment them? Indeed, it tells them that a sincere repentance will, even at the moment of death, disarm celestial wrath and purify the filthy souls of sinners. In some superstitions, priests lay claim to the right to forgive the dying of the sins committed during the course of a disorderly life, thereby pardoning the punishment due. The most evil of individuals, who have been encouraged in immorality, approved of in wickedness, and supported in crime, count on being aided by superstition and religion. They are promised reconciliation with the Divinity whom they have irritated, thereby avoiding the rigorous punishments for the enormity of sins they've committed. As a result of the ease with which one can be forgiven, which neutralizes fears and seems so favorable to the wicked, far from correcting behavior instead encourages one to persist in the most evil of acts right up to the moment of death. And despite the advantages proposed by the doctrine of a life to come, and in defiance of its supposed ability to repress our passions, don't the priest themselves complain constantly about its failure? They acknowledge that mortals who have been programmed since infancy with these ideas are weak and have a propensity for evil. They complain of humans being slaves to their pleasures, controlled by bad habits, driven by the world around them, and seduced by their present interests, all which make them forget equally about the rewards and punishments of a future existence. In other words, the interpreters of superstition, the ministers of religions, admit that their followers, for the most part, conduct themselves in this world as if they have nothing to fear or hope for in the next.

Let's pretend that the doctrine of eternal punishment was useful in that it really restrained a small number of individuals. Now compare these feeble advantages to the countless evils that flow from it. For every timid person who this idea restrains, there are thousands who it has no effect on, and thousands more who it makes irrational, turning them into savage killers and fanatics. It disturbs the minds of many, diverting them from their duties to society. And there are infinitely many more for whom it produces grief without bringing any real good for them or their associates.

Yet many look at those who do not believe in this philosophy as enemies of society. History shows us that the most enlightened individuals from the past and of the present, not only believe that the soul is material and perishes with the body, but that the idea of everlasting punishment has no merit but to strike fear into our hearts. We can also look at the number of systems created to establish the immortality of the soul as evidence of the futility of this doctrine, especially when the natural and just implications to be drawn from them are examined. The most Godly and virtuous people of current and ancient societies have done so. Some ancients professed that the doctrine of future punishments was fabulous, solely meant for the imbecility of the uninformed, but not created for those who cultivate their reason. Others expressly state that "man has neither good to hope nor evil to fear after death." Still others treat the torments of Hell as fables and view death as the end of everything for man. Some passages contemplate death as a state of total annihilation. Some societies, who made the soul immortal, had no idea of future punishments, because the soul returned to the divinity after death. Other philosophers had the same idea with a different twist here or there. So, as the hour of death approaches, do not think about evil or make things worse than they are. Instead think of them as they really are. The time has come when the elements that you are composed of will return to their original state. What is so terrible or grievous about that? Is there anything in the world that perishes totally? The fact is that what happens to us happens to all beings and eventually all will die. It is only vanity that makes us think we will have a life after death. All start as dust and return to dust. We should take pride in our accomplishments because they are our contribution. Even the bible, which was supposedly inspired by the Divinity states in the third chapter of Genesis, "In the sweat of your face you will eat bread until you return to the ground that you were made from: you were made from dust and to dust you will return."

Chapter 14

Education, Morals, and Laws Suffice to Restrain Us; The Desire of Immortality; Suicide

Motives that will make us act in a virtuous manner will not be found in an ideal world that exists only in the imagination, but instead in this, the visible world. It is within Nature, experience, and truth that we must look for remedies for the evils of our species and for motives that will infuse the human heart with ideas and actions that are truly useful to society.

Above all, it is *education* that will provide the means of identifying errors and showing the solutions to problems that have plagued mankind. It is this that should help sensible beings form habits that are advantageous to society and beneficial to individuals. This will help us see that there is no need for celestial punishments in order for us to learn the value of virtue. We do not need to fear the torments of hell as a means of directing us from a life of crime. Nature can teach us what we owe ourselves far better than a bunch of fables. Laws should point out what we owe the society of which we are a member. Education grounded in truth and usefulness will form citizens that are of value to the state. Government should guide the educational process to assure that each individual can be a contributing member of society. Those whose actions are harmful to society should be punished. Citizens should be able to see the rewards of a good education and the punishments associated with a lack of morals. In a state that is well formed and governed, all citizens can see that *virtue* is the only true road to happiness, that *talents* are the way to earn respect, that lack of *usefulness* leads to misfortune, and that *crime* leads to contempt.

A just, enlightened, virtuous, and vigilant government, which honestly looks after the public good, will have no need for fables or falsehoods to govern reasonable citizens. It should be shamed if it tries to deceive the public by misusing the power it has to direct its subjects. Citizens know it is in their best interest to submit to equitable laws and can feel the benefits of doing so. Regarding punishments, good governments understand that habits instill enough horror to deter most from committing crimes. Also, the visible punishments of this world are far more effective in deterring crime than those of a distant future. In other words, the sensible benefits and punishments of a well governed society touch the imagination of mortals far more effectively than the vague rewards and penances that are promised as part of a life after death. Also, those who respond to the idea of future rewards and punishments would be even more inclined to virtue if they thought they'd be rewarded in the present as well as in the future.

In so many cases we reject reason because we are not governed according to our Nature and we do not know her necessary laws. In most societies, we are fed superstitious fantasies by authority figures who neglect our instruction and seek to deceive us. All over the world we see leaders who are corrupted by the power of money and have little interests in the welfare of the people they govern. They are indifferent about their duties to the public and entirely focused on their duties to wealthy people and corporations that helped them attain their positions of power. Instead of building nations, they frequently work to destroy nations through never ending wars. They become blind to objects important to the happiness of their nations. These weak leaders are only interested in maintaining their sources of power, viewing anything that tries to address their misdeeds as a threat. They are, in their present state, deprived of the understanding which teaches us that it is in our interest to be kind, just, and virtuous. Instead, in their demented state, they reward only crimes that they imagine as useful to them. Generally, they punish the virtuous people whose actions go against their own imprudent passions, but which reason point outs to be truly beneficial to the interests of the society and themselves. Under such leadership is it surprising that cities and states become dysfunctional? At every level of such a culture, oppression and hostility become the norms, and most lose sight of the true path to happiness. Evil leaders gain power by pitting each of the members of a society against one another. We are wicked, not because we are born that way, but because we are rendered so. The impoverished and unhappy in a society are frequently crushed with indifference by the powerful, both at home and abroad. To save their lives they seek to retaliate, either openly or in secret, against the leadership, who to them is a step-mother, who gives all to some and nothing to others. In many cases they use the afterlife as a motivation to attack with impunity. For them, the punishments of this world pale in comparison to necessity. All is created by corrupt leaders and the failure to properly educate.

Many countries neglect morals because they want the populace to be timid and miserable, making most slaves to the state. Out of necessity, citizens become corrupt, absorbed, suppressed, and without honor in a world where all they have are the vices of the state. Everywhere we look we are deceived, encouraged in ignorance, and prevented from cultivating our reason. When we see vice applauded and crime honored we become stupid, irrational, and wicked, as we conclude vice to be good and virtue a useless sacrifice of self. We are miserable in so many ways that we resort to injuring our fellow-beings in a fruitless attempt to relieve our own anguish. Showing us heaven in hopes of restraining us does not work, since we can only focus on our earthly existence. We want happiness no matter what the price, which makes laws that don't provide for our knowledge, morale, or happiness, a useless menace. Recklessly, we pursue our necessities which eventually lead to punishment, all due to the unjust negligence of legislators. There would be less crime if: enlightened politics focused on instruction, welfare, and equitable laws; society cared for all its members by provided quality education as well as the assistance that all have a right to expect; and governments were less greedy, more vigilant, and determined to make their subjects happy. Society would not have to destroy lives to punish wickedness, which is usually caused by vices within the institution. Also, there would be no need to seek another life for fanciful illusions, which always give way to real wants and passions. If people were well educated they'd be happier. Politics would no longer be reduced to the need of deceiving the public in order to restrain them. The incarceration of so many unfortunates for crimes against their fellow beings would be greatly reduced.

Truth will always be the foundation on the path to enlightenment. Instead of kindling the imagination with ideas of punishments that await us after death, we should be comforted and supported, or at least we should be able to enjoy the fruits of our labor. Instead of being ravished to the core by cruel shams, or driven to unemployment and idleness because we cannot support ourselves and our families, which will surely lead to crime, we must be guided to consider our present existence, without having to worry about what will happen to us after death. Instead, we should be excited to productivity and our talents rewarded in a society that allows each individual to be active, working, kind, and virtuous. An added benefit is that our actions will have an influence over fellow-citizens. Instead of being menaced with the tortures of another world, we should be able to live in a world of peace, where we can plainly see the consequences of hatred, and the values of affection and self-esteem. To acquire self-esteem we must have virtue, knowing that the virtuous individual has nothing to fear and everything for which to hope.

If it is desired to form honest, courageous, and industrious citizens, who will be useful to their country, then beware of inspiring people from infancy with an unfounded fear of death. Don't fill the imagination with marvelous fables which occupy the mind with a destiny in a future life, which is useless information and has nothing to do with real happiness. Instead teach the public about the kind of immortality that is earned by courageous and noble souls who spend their physical and intellectual energy working toward the betterment of mankind in the present and for generations to come. Indeed, this is an immortality which genius, talent, and above all virtue, have a right to invent. These natural passions which will make people happy and result in positive contributions to society must never be stifled.

The idea of death along with the loss of the ability to communicate and influence fellow-beings is extremely painful, especially for those who have a passionate imagination. The *desire of immortality*, or living in the memory of our fellow beings, was always the passion and motivation of individuals who have played a great part on earth. *Heroes*, whether virtuous or criminal, *philosophers* as well as *conquerors, men of genius* and *men of talents*, those sublime personalities that have done honor to their species, as well as those illustrious villains who have corrupted and ravaged it, have had an eye to posterity in all their endeavors. They have flattered themselves with the hope of influencing the souls of humans, even when they no longer exist. Even the person who does not think about passing views to future generations can see regeneration in offspring, who will pass on a name and preserve the memory of the parents. It is for them that we build a house or plant a tree that may survive long after we are gone so they can live happily as a result of our labors. The thought of being entirely forgotten is a fear that embitters the life of those who are useless to the world, many times the very wealthy. They fear that the useless person dies entirely. The idea that one will be thought of in a favorable manner is a useful illusion and a vision that can flatter even those who know nothing will come from it. We enjoy dreaming that we will have power and a place in the universe, even after we cease to exist. We imagine being part of projects, actions, and discussions in future societies, and would be very unhappy if we thought ourselves to be excluded. The laws in all countries have adopted these views to the extent that they give the dying the ability to exercise their will long after death. It has gone to the extent that the dead frequently control the condition of the living for generations. Proof is seen in *pyramids, mausoleums, monuments,* and *epitaphs,* all which show our desire to prolong our existence beyond death. Knowing that posterity will judge us, we envisions philosophers writing about us, monarchs erecting grand palaces to honor us, and virtuous citizens appealing to us for justice from prejudice contemporaries. Such happy fantasies, generous illusions, and mild visions, the powers of which are so consoling and bland, come to life in zealous imaginations. This desire in us gives birth to, as well as sustains and nurtures, a mature enthusiasm of genius, devotion to courage, greatness of souls, and the perfection of talent. Its force is so gentle and its influence is so pleasing that it sometimes restrains the most powerful individuals, who experience has frequently shown to be very concerned about how they will be judged by posterity, from imposing suffering on individuals or large groups of people.

To some degree, all of us care about how we will be remembered after death. We all want to be remembered in a positive light. Is there anyone who, after death, would not like to excite emotions in survivors, influencing their thoughts, moving their souls, and exercising power over them, even from the grave? Those superstitious beings, timid people, and furious bigots who denounce this sentiment, which is so important to citizens and societies, must be ignored. We must not listen to the passionless philosophers who want to smother this noble spring of the soul. These skeptics will try to seduce us with sarcasm by pretending to despise an immortality that they did not invent. Yet the idea of being remembered for generations to come is a respectable and admirable motive when one's actions have a positive influence over contemporaries and perhaps even nations not yet formed. We should respect the enthusiasm of those good people, those mighty geniuses, and those stupendous talents, whose keen and penetrating insights have helped us by: providing for our welfare and happiness; securing our freedom; writing for us; enriching us through their discoveries; and curing us of some of our errors. We should pay them the homage they deserve, or at least respect their memory for the benefits we have derived from them. When we enjoy the pleasures and experience the happiness they worked to provide for us, we should remember them with gratitude. Through it all, we can learn from these great people the value of reason while avoiding others mistakes that were the result of superstitious fanaticism. We will recognize political intolerance as bad and virtue as praise worthy. We will never seek to persecute other for possessing views that are different than ours.

We should remember with reverence the immortal shades of those happy geniuses whose works excite the fondest of sentiments and who were the delight of the human race. We must know that in order to be remembered by our fellow beings and the generations to follow we must display talents, exhibit integrity, and practice virtue. It is rare to see a tear shed at the funeral of a vicious leader who excited terror in those who live under him. Tremble cruel leaders who plunge your subjects into misery, who ravage nations, and who change the fruitful earth into a barren cemetery; tremble for the bloody traits that historians will present to future generations, yet unborn, as your legacy. Neither your splendid monuments, nor your imposing victories, nor your countless armies, nor your boot-licking leeches can prevent posterity from avenging their grandfathers by treating your disgusting memories with scorn and showing nothing but contempt for your great crimes.

Even though death is anticipated with pain by most, we usually hope others will take interest in the fact that we've died. For this to happen in a positive light, the deceased must have exhibited talent and been a person of virtue. It should come as no surprise that many spend much of their time absorbed by their own vanity, working toward the possession of foolish objects, and satisfying their vile passions, often at the expense of family, friends, and society. How are such people remembered by their survivors? There are many leaders of nations that history tells us nothing about except that they lived. Despite the uselessness that makes up most lives, all want their death to be interesting to the point that the natural order of things should be overturned at that time. O mortal, feeble and vain! Don't you know that all the leaders from the past are dead, yet the universe has not stopped? The death of those famous conquerors that enslaved mortals was the cause of happiness for the entire human race. Do you foolishly believe that your talents are of interest to the human species and that they are sufficient to cause the world to mourn at your decease? So many who have made significant contributions to the human race die without notice or care by most of their fellow citizens. Dare you flatter yourself that your reputation, titles, riches, extravagant banquets, and varied pleasures will make your funeral a sad event? Don't be surprised that your name may be spoken for a few days and nothing more. Know that many have died before you who were more illustrious, powerful, wealthy, and hedonistic than you, and you did not even know they existed. So, be a virtuous person, in whatever station life assigns you, and you will be happy, good, cherished, talented, and respected over the course of your lifetime. Posterity will admire you if your talents are beneficial to the interests of those to follow, at which time they may associate a name with those benefits. Also know that the universe will not be disturbed by your loss, and while your family and friends sadly lean over to close your eyes, your nearest neighbor may well be celebrating with joy!

Instead of worrying about what will happen to us after death, or how we will be remembered, we should diligently work to make ourselves useful to those closest to us. For our own happiness we should take care of our parents, be faithful to spouses, attentive to children, kind to relations, true to friends, and fair to employees if a business owner. In these ways we will be admirable in the eyes of our fellow citizens. We should give what is due to our country because it guarantees our welfare. The desire of pleasing posterity should excite us to positive labors that will elicit the eulogies of our countrymen. We should learn to love ourselves knowing that self-esteem never comes when concealed vices and sacred crimes degrade us in our own eyes, making us ashamed of our own conduct. This mindset will allow us to contemplate death with the same indifference with which most of our fellow beings will view it. We should expect death with steadiness, waiting for it with calm resignation, ignoring the vain terrors with which superstition has tried to overwhelm us. This way we can leave vague hopes to the believers, speculations to the mad-brained fanatics, and fears to the bigots. As such, the heart, which was strengthened by reason and validated by love of virtue, no longer needs to dread a dissolution that will destroy all feeling.

Regardless of our attachment to life and the fear of death, every day we see that habit, opinion, and prejudice are sufficient motives, causing us to forget about these passions and make us brave danger, putting our existence in jeopardy. Ambition, pride, jealousy, love, vanity, greed, the desire for glory, or admiration of opinion that recognizes us with honor, all have the ability to make us shut our eyes to danger, to laugh at peril, and push us to death. Anger, anxiety of mind, disgrace, and want of success soften the idea of death. It becomes a door that will shelter us from the injustices of mankind. Poverty, trouble, and adversity make death appear to be a reasonable option. The unfortunate embrace it in despair when unhappy and without resources. Shamefulness accelerates its march when one believes happiness is no longer attainable.

At different times in different countries societies formed a variety of opinions about those who had the boldness to put an end to their own existence. Ideas on this subject, like all others, have been molded by religions, governed by superstitious systems, and modified by political institutions. The Greeks, the Romans, and other nations, where courage and nobility were honored, contemplated as Gods those who voluntarily cut the thread of life. There was a time when women of India were inspired to burn themselves on the dead bodies of their husbands. And the Japanese, for the most trivial of reasons, had no problem plunging a dagger into his bosom. Christianity in most of its forms teaches that it is offensive to the Deity to commit suicide. Some moralists, hypothesizing the height of religious ideas, say it is never permitted for us to break our bond with society. Others view suicide as an act of cowardice saying it's a weakness to use it to avoid the overwhelming shafts of destiny. They say it is much more courageous, and elevating to the soul, to deal with ones afflictions and accept the blows of fate.

If we look to Nature at this point we will see that all the actions of people, feeble playthings in the hands of necessity, are unchangeable. Our actions depend on causes which move us despite ourselves and without our knowledge. In each moment of life we are accomplishing another of the decrees of Nature. The same power that obliges all intelligent beings to cherish their existence also makes life so painful and cruel that some quit the species. When order is destroyed, a decree of Nature that wills the end of existence is accomplished. This Nature has worked for thousands of years to form in the bowels of the earth the iron that must number our days.

Our relationship with Nature is not the result of a choice that either one makes. Our will had nothing to do with our birth and frequently we finish life in conflict with the will. Recall that our actions are the necessary effects of unknown causes which determine the will. We are in the hands of

Nature, like a sword in our own hand, which cannot accuse us or our hand for misusing it. We can only love our existence when we are happy. When everything makes us sad and we can only imagine negative outcomes, at that point we cease to exist. Suspended in a void and overwhelmed with disaster we cannot be useful to ourselves or others.

The bonds between citizens and society are conditional contracts that must be beneficial to all parties involved. Citizens are bound to country and associates by the promise of happiness. But what happens when these bonds are broken? Do the representatives of society treat us with harsh injustice, making our existence painful? Are we disgraced or forsaken with adversity? Is our family life miserable or does our happiness depend on objects we cannot attain? For whatever the reasons, one quits a home, society, country, or world that holds no promise. Death appears to be the only remedy for despair to this sad individual as the sword becomes a friend. If we see the slightest ray of hope, we will not terminate our existence. When a ray of hope cannot be seen, living is the greatest evil and death the way to avoid the excess of despair. This has been the opinion of many great people who chose death over the life of a slave or who gave their life for the sake of their country and are viewed as hero's. Such individuals prefer quitting the world rather than living in one that does not support or allow for their happiness.

A society that cannot or is not willing to provide any benefits to its people loses all its rights over them. When Nature renders our existence completely miserable she is, in fact, ordering us to quit it. In dying we do no more than fulfill one of her decrees, just as we did when we drew our first breath. For the individual who does not fear death and who hangs on to life, that person will call on resources that Nature has given us to stay alive. Nature has not abandoned us if we can still experience pleasure and see an end to our pain.

We judge our fellow beings based on our feelings. We see violence as an act of confusion which is not appropriate and which is meant to deprive us of our happiness. We see others as weak when they do not have the same strength we exhibit or think we would display when it comes to resisting temptations. We view the individual who commits suicide as mad because we think of life as a great blessing, especially when we think the reason for such an act is trivial. This is how we make ourselves judges over the happiness of others thinking we know how others see and feel their world. The miser who commits suicide after losing everything appears a fool to one who is not attached to wealth. We do not understand that to the miser, life without money is torture, and nothing in the world can take away this persons feeling of pain. We would say that had we been in the place of the miser we would not have done the same, but we could never have the same temperament, passions, ideas, and circumstances to make such a decision. If we did, we would make the same decision once deprived of the only source of happiness we have. When a person decides to commit suicide, an act that goes against our natural tendencies, this individual feels that nothing in the world can bring about happiness. When one loses all hope and believes that there are no cures, reason can no longer guide this person. Whatever the misfortunes may be, to the individual they are real, and whether we view it as strong or weak, the final decision belongs to the individual. Even the person who only imagines being sick still suffers considerably. So, when someone commits suicide it should be concluded that life had become too much to bear, that it had lost all its charm and that nature could not offer any form of relief. When a disturbed imagination compared existence with non-existence the latter appeared preferable.

Many who don't believe suicide is ever a proper response will consider these views as dangerous. Nevertheless, it's a temperament that comes from sorrow, anger, habit, organization, and defective thinking. We necessarily view our own self-destruction as an act that defies reason. We would never consider such an act as long as we have hope for the future. If we see no hope we have no interest in preserving our life. Frequently, those who feel this way would have ultimately been removed from society for offensive actions.

If life is our greatest blessing it must be presumed that the act of suicide is moved by an invincible force. It is the excess of misery, the height of despair, and the derangement of the brain that urge a person to commit suicide. Upset by contrary impulses, we are obliged to follow a middle course that leads to death. We are never a free-agent in life, especially when we terminate our existence. It will be seen that the individual who commits suicide does not, as is pretended, commit an act against nature. This person follows an impulse which defies reason and adopts the only means left to quit seemingly endless pain. We go out a door which nature leaves open for us. We cannot offend in accomplishing a law of necessity.

The iron hand that made life desirable and urged self-conservation will show the way to quit a system that has become too miserable. Our country or our family has no right to complain if they have no way to make us happy and we have nothing left to offer them.

It is useful for society to inspire us with a love of life and banish false ideas about death and its consequences from the mind. Fear of death creates cowards and fear of its consequences creates fanatics or sad beings that are useless to themselves and unprofitable to others. Death is a resource that should not be taken away when virtue, which the injustices of a society frequently reduce to despair, is oppressed. If we feared death less we would not be a slave or superstitious. Truth would find zealous defenders and the rights of mankind would be upheld with conviction. Virtue would be boldly maintained and error would be more powerfully opposed. Tyranny, which cowardice nourishes and fear perpetuates, would be banished from nations. In fact, *we can neither be contented nor happy while our opinions make us tremble.*

Chapter 15

Our True Interest = Our Happiness; We Cannot Be Happy Without Virtue

As has been said before, the only way we should be judged is by how useful our contributions were, or are, toward the happiness of our fellow-beings. The harmful person is always looked down upon. Understanding this we will now look at principles that are either useful or useless to the human race. If we are always moving toward our own happiness, we can only approve of objects that help us attain it. Happiness can only be realized when the impressions, perceptions, and ideas, or the motions excited in us by an object, are in sync with our organization, conformable to our temperament, and integrated with our individual nature. Modified by habit and formed by an infinity of circumstances, it is necessary that the action of the object that moves us, or the idea of it, should strengthen us instead of making us weak or destroying our feelings. It's necessary that the object excite activity in the body and mind without fatiguing the mind, exhausting the body, or harming the organs. What is the object that combines all these qualities? Where is the individual who can be continuously exited to action without pain or fatigue? We enjoy exerting the body and pushing its limits, as long as we can do so without extreme pain. Frequently we agree to suffer rather than not feel at all. We learn to enjoy things that are initially disagreeable, but eventually convert themselves into wants, or until they no longer have an effect on us. Tobacco, coffee, and above all alcohol, are examples of this. Some run to see an accident or watch other gruesome activities because of this conversion. Our desire to feel and be moved in a powerful way is a function of the principle of curiosity. Because of this, we enthusiastically seize the marvelous, or sincerely cling to the supernatural, or display a temperament for the incomprehensible. But where in nature can we find objects that will continuously supply the needed stimulus to keep us active, yet maintain the balance required by our organization, which is in a constant state of change? The liveliest pleasures are always the most short-lived because they exhaust us the most.

For one to be happy all the time is impossible. It would require the possession of infinite individual powers and a disposition that nothing could change, or that objects would change their properties to be in agreement with such a person. Since we are constantly changing due to causes that we are not aware of, and despite ourselves, the thought that objects around us would be able to anticipate such changes is absurd. This is why objects that please us in one season displease us in another. The objects themselves have not sensibly changed, but our organs, disposition, ideas, mode of seeing, and manner of feeling have changed. Such is the source of our inconsistency.

If one object cannot make one individual happy all the time, it is easy to see that that object is even less likely to bring happiness, or the same degree of happiness, to all individuals. Beings, so different in so many ways and for reasons like, temperament, faculties, organization, imagination, ideas, opinions, and habits, all of which are modified by an infinity of circumstances, must form very different notions of happiness. The happiness of each individual is a consequence of one's natural organization, and of the circumstances, habits, and ideas, be they true or false, that have modified the individual. Since the organization and circumstances are never the same for any two humans, it follows that something that makes one person happy will be indifferent or even displeasing to another. So, as we have said before, no one can truly judge as to what will contribute to the happiness of one's fellow beings.

The welfare of an individual, which is based on temperament and ideas, is referred to as *interest* and is nothing more that which the person believes is necessary to create a feeling of happiness. It must be concluded that all people have interests. The miser wants to amass wealth while the wasteful wants to spend it all. The interest of the ambitious is to obtain power while the modest philosopher seeks to enjoy tranquility. The hedonist wants to give in to all sorts of pleasures while the prudent person wants to abstain from those pleasures that will result in injury. The interest of the wicked is to gratify individual passions at any price while the virtuous person strives to earn self-esteem as well as the esteem and love of others through personal actions. When it is said that *Interest is the only motive of human actions*, it means that each of us works toward our own happiness in our own way. Whether our interests are visible or hidden, or real or imaginary, one's whole system of conduct is directed toward its attainment. Every person has interests and if we feel that someone has no interests it's because we are ignorant of that person's motives. Someone may not appear to have an interest in personal happiness when that individual devotes time and money toward helping the less fortunate. All people who place their happiness in making sacrifices are viewed as uninterested in their own happiness by those who don't see value in the sacrifice being made. We frequently, and incorrectly, judge the interests of others because the motivations for those interests are too hard to understand. Indeed, in order to be able to judge fairly it's necessary to have the same eyes, organs, passions, and opinions as the person being judged. Nevertheless, we must form judgments of the actions of mankind by their effects on us. We approve of the interests that move us to action whenever the result is advantageous to our species. So, we admire valor, generosity, the love of liberty, great talents, virtue, etc. and we approve of the objects that have led to the happiness of the beings that exemplified those qualities. Sometimes we approve without being able to feel the effects because it fits our interest. Experience, reflection, habit, and reason have given us a taste for morals so that we can take pleasure in being witness to a great and generous action. The person who has made a habit of practicing virtue is one who has earned the esteem and support of others, as well as a sense of self-esteem and self-love. We abstain from acts that are malicious or criminal because they would degrade us in our own eyes. We are like someone who has learned the habit of cleanliness from infancy and is disgusted at being dirty, even if no one can see it. The honest individual is one whose interests, or happiness, is shown in actions that others are obliged to love because this persons actions are in their interest.

These principles, when worked on and developed, are the true basis of morals. Nothing is more fanciful than principles that are based on imaginary motives which have no foundation in nature, or that rely on instinctive views which some feel are outside of our experience and are independent of the advantages we gain from their use. It is our essence to love ourselves which is why we tend to our own conservation and seek to live in happiness. So, our interest, or the desire to be happy, is the only real motive for all our actions. This interest depends on our natural organization, our wants, our acquired ideas, and the habits we have contracted. We are undoubtedly in error when a weakened organization or false opinions lead us to believe we will find happiness in objects that are either useless or injurious to us or others. Conversely, we march on paths of virtue and our own happiness when true ideas guide us to conduct that is useful to our species. Only then will we gain approval and earn the admiration of our associates. *Morals* would be a vain science if it did not undoubtedly prove to us that our *interests consist in being virtuous*. Our commitments must be based on the probability, or the certainty, of either obtaining a good or avoiding an evil.

Indeed, a sensible and intelligent being is always working toward self-preservation and individual welfare, and although we are responsible for our own happiness, experience quickly proves to us that we cannot attain it alone. In order to acquire all the objects necessary for our happiness we must seek the aid of our fellow beings. We live with sensible, intelligent beings that, like ourselves, are seeking their own happiness and might be able to help us attain the objects we desire. We may find that we are not always in agreement with these other beings but our happiness will demand that we conduct ourselves in a manner that will endear us to those who, by working together, can acquire mutual benefits from their relationship. We realize that we are most necessary to the welfare of each other and to get the advantages of human relations both parties must make strides toward their own happiness. So, to give real advantages to beings of the human species is to have virtue. The reasonable person must feel that it is worth the effort to be virtuous. *Virtue is the art of rendering ones-self happy, by contributing to the felicity of others*. The virtuous person communicates happiness to those beings who can return the feeling of happiness, who are necessary to self-conservation, and who will make existence peaceful.

Merit and virtue, which are basic to our nature, and are dependent on our desires, are the true foundation of all morals. It is virtue alone that can make us truly happy. A society without virtue cannot be useful and can only exist on a superficial level. A society is only useful when it brings together beings who have a desire to help each other and who are willing to work toward the advantage of all. There is no comfort within families whose members are not in a position to help and support each other through hard times. Wedded bonds are sweet only when they are between two individuals who are united by the want of legitimate pleasure. From these unions come the means to form political societies and provide them with citizens. Friendships are useful when two virtuous beings have a sincere desire of working toward their reciprocal happiness. It is only through the display of virtue that we can show and value goodness, win confidence, and gain the admiration of all our relations. No one can be independently happy.

The happiness of each human individual depends on the views we adopt and the feelings we nourish in the beings with which destiny has placed us. One may dazzle fellow beings with grandeur, or demand involuntary service and obedience through force and power, or seduce some with wealth, but it is humanity, benevolence, compassion, and fairness that, without assistance or effort, will attain the esteem of reasonable beings. To be virtuous, one must take an interest in the interests of others and enjoy the benefits of helping fellow beings realize their own form of happiness. When our nature, education, reflections, and habits make us capable of being virtuous, and circumstances give us the opportunity to be so, we become interesting to all who come into contact with us. We see and enjoy the happiness we helped to create in our family, friends, and fellow workers. We live in peace knowing that we have helped to make the world a better place. Our happiness and self-love become a hundred times better when we see them shared by all with whom we have come in contact. The habit of virtue creates no wants except for the ones it satisfies. It is therefore true that *virtue is always its own peculiar reward.* It recompenses itself with all the advantages which it continually obtains for others.

Some will say, rightfully so, that in the world in which we live, virtue, instead of creating happiness in the lives of those who practice it, frequently results in misfortune and almost everywhere goes unrewarded. A thousand examples could be offered as evidence that in almost every country it's hated, persecuted, and forced to suffer the ingratitude of human nature. I reply with conviction that it is a necessary consequence of the errors of the human race. Virtue rarely leads us to objects that will lead us away from happiness. Many societies are frequently ruled by leaders whose ignorance makes them abuse their power and whose prejudices make them enemies of virtue. Such leaders, flattered by boot-lickers and secure that their actions will never lead to prosecution, commonly reward none but the most unworthy. But the truly honest person does not look for recognition from a society that is corrupt. We are content with the happiness we find at home and in our community. We do not seek to enhance dangerous relationships. We avoid evil and do as much good as possible within our sphere of influence. We watch as the wicked make life miserable for themselves and others and we cry for both. We applaud the mediocrity that affords us security. We pity the nations that are made miserable by their errors and unhappy as a consequence of their fatal but necessary passions. We see citizens who reject virtue, a quality that would lead to true happiness.

Saying that virtue is its own reward simply means that in a well formed society, one whose core values are guided by truth, trained by experience, and conducted by reason, we would know our true interests and the reasons for our associations. We would have meaningful motives for our contributions and would realize the advantages of fulfilling them. In fact, we would find happiness in helping others secure their own form of it. In a well-formed society the government, the laws, education, and example all work together to prove to citizens that they are part of a nation that is founded on virtue. The happiness of the whole is dependent upon virtue. Experience would continuously reaffirm that the welfare of the different parts of the society are dependent on the whole. Justice would be viewed as advantageous when it consistently shows that no society can help its members if the actions of a few are harmful to many.

Unfortunately, our errors have influenced and confused our ideas to the point where virtue has been and still is disgraced, banished, and persecuted. The advantages we have a right to expect are rarely seen and instead promised as rewards in a future life. It's thought to be okay, even necessary, to deceive, seduce, and intimidate us into following a virtue that is difficult at best. We are told to practice virtue with hope for a distant world while the world we live in is hateful. We are taught to fear distant terrors to keep us from committing evil acts. This is how politics and superstitions, formed by warped imaginations and created by fictitious interests, try to replace the real motives nature supplies and experience teaches. Enlightened governments would present truths to its citizens instead of deceiving them. Laws would enforce, instruction would sanction, example would encourage, and rational opinions would view a society guided by virtue as good for all citizens. Instead, blinded by passions, led by precedent, authorized by custom, and enslaved by habit, we pay no attention to the uncertainty of future promises regardless of the perils they hold. Interests in our immediate pleasure, the force of our passions, and deeply ingrained habits always supersede distant interests about our future welfare or the remote evils used to threaten us, which always appear doubtful when compared with present advantages.

So, *superstition, far from making us virtuous by principle, does nothing more than impose a yoke on us which is as severe as it is useless.* It is worn by none other than enthusiasts or the fearful who without becoming better, tremble as they bite the bit put into their mouth. Such people become either unhappy or dangerous. This is how superstition becomes a dyke that is too weak to resist the torrent of corruption to which so many causes give an irresistible force. Indeed, superstition results in public disorder by the dangerous passions it frees, by the conduct it sanctions, and by the actions it consecrates. In such an environment, virtue is confined to a few rational souls who have the strength of mind to resist the stream of prejudices. These people are content with the benefits they derive from being a good person in a corrupt society and the approval of a small number of virtuous people. The virtuous are detached from the useless advantages of being part of an unjust society that frequently rewards nothing but crime.

Despite the injustice that is seen all over the world, there are some virtuous people who survive in the most degenerate of nations. There are good leaders who are fully acquainted with the true value of virtue. They are smart enough to know that all, even enemies of the state, recognize and acknowledge it. They are able to rejoice in their own work, possessing contented minds and enjoying concealed pleasures that no earthly power can take away from them. The honest person earns respect, wins confidence, and gains the love of all, even those whose actions are the opposite. In other words, vice will always be embarrassed by, and unwillingly acknowledge, the superiority of virtue. And even when it seems that the whole universe has turned against honest individuals, they have the sublime advantage of loving their own conduct. There is no power that can take that away from them just as there is no power that can give it to them if it is not earned. When people are honored for evil acts it is not wisdom but extreme folly which should be stopped. Indeed this *vanity and vexation of spirit* is nothing more than ARROGANCE. Yet when such praise is based on talents and actions useful to the community, when it is based on virtue, it should be recognized as NOBLE PRIDE, ELEVATION OF MIND, and GRANDEUR OF SOUL.

And what are the consequences of listening to those superstitious beings who are not only enemies of our happiness but who wish to destroy it in the innermost recesses of the heart? What happens to us when we are told that we are born with original sin? What happens when we are told that we must hate certain groups of people? All is an attempt to steal the self-respect of honest people which is frequently the only reward of being virtuous in a backward world. To destroy our sense of justice and our ability to love ourselves is to weaken a most powerful stimulus that moves us to do good for our fellow mortals. What other motive can there be but control of the greater part of human societies? Under these conditions virtue is discouraged, honesty is condemned, daring crimes are encouraged, elusive conspiracy is praised, cunning vice is rewarded, love of public work is viewed as stupid, precision in fulfilling duties is unimportant, and compassion is belittled. ARE TRAITORS DISTINGUISHED WITH PUBLIC HONORS? Yes, the consequences of allowing superstitious beings to rule our societies are that a lack of morals is applauded, deep feelings are mocked, and tenderness is ridiculed. All the while seduction, meanness, treacherous faith, greed, and fraud run rampant and are viewed as acceptable by much of the world. We must have motives for our actions which are either good or evil based on what we believe will make us happy. When we judge something will move us toward happiness we believe it to be in our interest. We do nothing freely. When we are not rewarded for useful actions we are reduced to feelings as helpless as those of our peers or we quietly reward ourselves with our own applause.

Knowing this, we conclude that we can never be completely unhappy or deprived of the rewards that we have earned. Virtue will always repay us for the good we do for others even when public opinion is against us. *Nothing can make up for a lack of virtue.* In the real world honest people, like the wicked, are not exempt from problems. We may experience physical problems, or live in poverty, or lack friendships, or be the victim of injustice, ingratitude or hatred, but through it all we will always be at peace with ourselves. We live with respect and dignity, consoled with the confidence inspired by the justice of our causes. We are happy with ourselves in the saddest of circumstances. The same cannot be said for the wicked person who, equally submitted to the destinies of a changing world, lives with regret and remorse in the deepest recesses of the heart and mind. Even for the psychopaths and sociopaths among us maddening anguish shows him his own deformities every time he sees his reflection, as he recalls his evil deeds with a memory that is too faithful. His own unruly passions take their toll on his body and his mind until he is taken over by despair and only death can relieve his anguish. The honest person is not immune to misfortune but can accept it without despair. If taken over by sickness this person has less to complain about than the vicious individual who is weakened by time. If we are poor, we are happier in our poverty. If we are disgraced we can endure it with strength and are not overwhelmed like the vile slave to crime.

So, the happiness of each individual depends on how ones temperament is formed. Nature makes both the happy and the unhappy. Culture gives ones temperament value while instruction makes it productive and reflection makes it useful. Nature gives the happy individual a sound body, a just mind, and passions that fit the person's situation in life. These combine with the energy to obtain those things which our station in life, our mode of thinking, and our temperament, render desirable. Nature gives the unhappy individual the fatal gift of a hot temper, or an overactive imagination, or rash desires for objects that are improper or impossible to obtain without placing one's welfare or the welfare of others in jeopardy. The happiest individual possesses a peaceful soul and only desires things that can be attained through labor that is suitable to us and our associates and is not shocking, violent, or troublesome to us or society. The philosopher, who's not ambitious and is satisfied with a limited circle of friends, is more happily organized than the ambitious conqueror whose greedy imagination is reduced to despair by the knowledge that there is only one world to ravage. The individual who is born to be happy, that is who nature has made to be modified toward happiness, is someone who is not harmful to others. Society is generally disturbed by those who are born into unhappiness and whose organization makes them wild. Such people are not happy with their destiny and they become drunk with their own passions. They often seek to set the world on fire, inflicting a heavy curse on mankind, all in order to attain imaginary benefits which they believe will make them happy. To satisfy his passion for glory, an Alexander's over active imagination falsely lead him to believe that he would find happiness via the destruction of empires, the burning of cities to the ground, and the killing of countless numbers of people. Others will seek a simpler life and find happiness without earthly possessions while a Socrates will want nothing more than the pleasure of forming discipline to virtue.

Motion is necessary and something we always desire. For this reason we become good at obtaining the objects we desire at which point they lose their interest to us. To feel happiness we must put forth some effort to obtain the objects we desire. We do not enjoy the things that come easily as much as those for which we must work. The brain puts the body into motion when it is motivated with the expectation of happiness, the labor required to get it, and the prospects it presents via the many pictures the imagination provides. We move into an agreeable activity for the enjoyment of happiness that it brings. Action is a true function of the human mind. When it ceases to act it is no longer useful. The entire being is affected by the actions of the mind. The impulses we get from our desires are a great benefit and are to the mind what exercise is to the body. Without our desires we would find little pleasure in the challenges presented to us. For example, thirst makes the pleasure of drinking so much more enjoyable. Life is a perpetual circle of regenerated desires and wants satisfied. Rest is most pleasing after work yet it's a curse to someone who has nothing to do. To enjoy without interruption is not to enjoy anything. The person who has nothing to desire is certainly less happy than the person who suffers.

These reflections, which are grounded in experience and truth, should prove that good as well as evil depend on the essence of things. To appreciate happiness one must labor creating a balance in life. The body must exercise, the heart must have desires, and the troubles we endure keep us in tune with our welfare and provide a true perspective to the picture of human life. It is an irrevocable law of our destiny that we are obliged to be discontent with our present condition, always making an effort to change it, and always seeking after a happiness that no individual enjoys perfectly. The pauper envies the affluence of the rich even though the latter is frequently less happy. The wealthy envy the middle class for the simplicity of the lives they lead, having less but needing less. If we were perfectly contented activity in the world would stop. We must desire so that we will act. We must work in order to be happy. It is the course of nature that life requires action. Human societies can only exist if there is a continuous exchange of those things that people rely on for happiness. The poor are obliged to desire and work to obtain the things they need to maintain their existence. The basic desires given to us by nature are the needs for food, clothing, lodging, and propagation of our species. When we have satisfied these we will quickly create entirely new desires or find ways to refine the basics giving them a fresh zest. When we have all that we desire we can no longer be happy unless we find ways to share our wealth. We will frequently hire others to work toward our welfare as they work toward theirs. Wants, always regenerating and never satisfied, are the principles of life, the soul of activity, the source of health, and the basis of society. If each individual could acquire personal happiness without the help of others, there would be no need for societies. But, our wants, desires, and whims put us in a state of dependence on others. This is why each individual's unique interests must be useful to others because they help each party get the things they need. A nation is nothing more than a conglomeration of people who connect with each other based on the reciprocity of their wants and their mutual desires for pleasure. The happiest people have the fewest wants and the most numerous means of satisfying them. The truly rich have no need to increase their fortune if they hope to have less wants.

The fact that wants change is absolutely necessary for individuals of the human species as well as for political societies. It is natural that once wants are satisfied they are replaced with wants labeled as *Imaginary or Fantasies*. These become as necessary to our happiness as the first. The want for clothing changes from civilization to civilization, season to season, and the poor to the wealthy. The very wealthy individual would be unhappy without a variety of clothes for every situation. As such vanity creates work for thousands of hands that are anxious to satisfy vain desires. Many others are able to satisfy their wants as a result of the wants of those who are more affluent. The wants of primitive civilizations was to hunt for food in forested areas. Over time their ancestors cleared woods and began growing and selling food. By degrees we refined our primitive wants, extended our sphere of action, gave birth to thousands of new wants, and imagined a thousand new ways to satisfy them. This is the natural course, the necessary progression, and the regular march of active beings who cannot live without feeling, and who, to be happy, must necessarily diversify their sensations. As our wants multiply, the means to satisfy them become proportionally more difficult and we must rely on more of our fellow beings. Our interests force us to engage others who agree with our view. Consequently, we must help them get the things they want. As each satisfies needs and desires the list of necessities grows. While the savage reaches for a piece of fruit to satisfy the need for nourishment, the rich person depends of the work of many across the globe to get the same sense of satisfaction. Riches are nothing more than the ability to use ones resources to put a large number of people to work to attain affluent wants. The trade-off is that many workers are moving toward the satisfaction of their specific interests. The individual of power offers happiness to many others in return for personal felicity.

The true sources of our misery are the false opinions we hold about our happiness. By seeking objects that are indifferent or useless to our welfare we lessen our chances of finding true contentment and instead bring evil and misfortune into our lives.

Riches are indifferent in themselves and it is only in the way they are used that they become useful or harmful.

Money is useless to the savage who does not understand its value. The miser saves it fearing that it might be spent on useless objects. In this day when people can use credit to spend money they do not have they frequently buy regret.

Pleasures mean nothing to the individual who cannot feel them. They become real evils when they are over indulged in, at which point they become destructive to our health or they make us neglect our duties or they make us hated by others.

Power is useless if we cannot use it to create our own individual happiness by increasing the happiness of the human species. Power becomes fatal when abused and detestable when used to make others miserable. It becomes a source of misery when it is stretched beyond nature's intended limits.

Because most people don't understand their true interests, the individual who finds happiness rarely discovers the secret of that happiness. One of the least understood arts is that of enjoying. We should learn this art before we begin to desire. The earth is covered by individuals who only care about getting "things," without ever understanding the true end result. The world is full of people who desire fortune, power, and pleasure, yet very few ever find true happiness. It is natural, reasonable, and necessary for us to desire those things that will increase the sum of our happiness. It's okay when we apply our ambition and most strenuous efforts toward the attainment of *power, riches,* and *pleasure* if we have learned how to use them to make our existence and that of those around us more agreeable. It's impossible to stop someone from desiring them or despising those who command them but when they are used to cause injury to one's self or others they become tools for injustice and evil and should be stopped. We should only have power, grandeur, and ambition when we can attain them without giving up our own sense of peace and that of those who surround us. We should only have riches that can be attained without incurring shame or the hatred of fellow beings but instead are used to increase personal happiness and that of others. We must always remember that personal happiness should be founded in self-esteem and the advantages we provide for others. Above all, we must never forget that of all the objects we desire, the most impractical for a being that lives in a society is *attempting to make ones-self exclusively happy.*

Chapter 16

Errors; What Constitutes Happiness; The True Source of Evil

Reason does not stop us from having big desires. Ambition is a useful passion when it is applied to obtaining the happiness of mankind. Great minds and elevated souls always want to extend their sphere of influence. Powerful geniuses, enlightened beings, and philanthropic people must spread their caring influence in order to make themselves happy while making countless others happy. So many people of wealth and power fail to enjoy true happiness because their feeble and narrow souls must act in a sphere too large for their energies. So, due to the laziness, passiveness, and ineffectiveness of leaders, nations frequently pine in misery, ruled by little minds that can't determine their own happiness let alone that of the people they govern. On the other hand, those leaders who are controlled by their passions are tormented by the narrow sphere that they live within and their aggression becomes a curse to the human race. Rulers on either side of this unfortunate coin are never in tune with their sphere of action.

Our happiness will always be a function of the harmony that exists between our desires and our circumstance. The power an individual leader possesses means nothing if it cannot be applied to the advantage of the governed which in turn would bring about the happiness of the leader. If the actions of the powerful are truly evil those actions make them miserable, and if they produce misfortune for some portion of the human race then such actions are detestable abuses. Most leaders don't know happiness. The people they rule are unfortunate because bad leaders focus on making themselves content without caring about citizens or because all they know about the general population are their response to abuse. A wise leader would be the happiest of mortals. The leader who is hated yet maintains an advantage over the population through subjugation, and whatever other unscrupulous methods are created to occupy a deprived mind, is the saddest of all individuals. The virtuous leader with an expansive mind uses power to gently unite and kindly consolidate the wills of authority with the wills of the governed. Respect, affection, and a positive place in the pages of history are earned through such actions. These are the conquests that reason offers to all who are destined to lead empires. Conquests grand enough to satisfy the most active imaginations yet sublime enough to please the largest ambition. Evil leaders see them as duties that must be fulfilled while true leaders are the happiest of individuals because they use their ambitions to make others happy which in turn brings happiness to them.

All who participate in the role of governing experience, to some degree, the advantages of the power associated with a position of leadership. As such, rank and reputation are legitimate goals for those who are in a position to use them in pursuit of their own happiness. They are useless to ordinary individuals who don't have the means to employ them in a way that is advantageous to themselves and others. Rank and reputation become detestable when a leader compromises personal happiness and the welfare of society. Society is in error anytime it respects leaders who use power for destructive purposes unless the end result substantially benefits all.

Riches, which can be harmful to many, in the hands of an honest individual can provide countless ways of enhancing happiness. But, before wishing for wealth one should know how to use it. Money is only a symbol of happiness. To enjoy it one must use it to make others happy. This is the great secret; the jewel; the reality! Money allows us to purchase those things which we desire yet the only thing it will not buy is *the knowledge of how to use it properly*. To have money without the knowledge of how to enjoy it is like having the key to a mansion that we are prohibited from entering. If we try to go inside we cause harm to ourselves and others. If we are enlightened with a sound mind and an extensive soul we will not be overwhelmed by wealth and power. Instead our benevolence will shine through earning us the respect, love, and praise of all who are within our sphere of influence. We will know that restraint is the only way to truly enjoy the pleasures we experience. We will know that all the treasures in the world cannot renew the mind, body, and soul, in short the senses, when they have been worn down by excess.

Any dogma that says it is wrong to seek power, wealth, or pleasure is nothing more than a superstitious rant. When a person has the ability to acquire them, these objects are desirable for humans, useful to society, and conducive to public happiness if they are used properly. An individual is on the right path when using reason, virtue, and truth as guides in the quest for more. If we harm no one and only use legitimate means to acquire the objects we desire, we will be applauded, respected, and loved because we will use them to secure our own happiness as well as that of our fellow beings. Pleasure is a loved and rational benefit when it makes one's existence really valuable and does not injure ones-self or others. *Riches* are a symbol that represents a majority of the benefits of this life. They become a reality in the hands of the people who know how to use them. *Power* is the brightest of all benefits when those who possess it have received from nature a noble soul, an elevated mind, a benevolent heart, and sufficient energy. These benefits must be combined with an education that taught a true regard for virtue and a love of truth that enables them to spread their happy influence over whole nations. At this point the masses are in a state of legitimate dependence on the will of the leader. *One only acquires the right of commanding others when rendering them happy.*

The right a human being has to rule over fellow beings can only be founded on the actual happiness secured for them or the promise of future happiness. Without real or promised happiness, the power exercised is violence, occupation, and manifest tyranny. Legitimate authority must be based on its ability to make others happy, without which it's nothing more than the *baseless fabric of a vision. No individual derives from nature the right of commanding another.* But it is voluntarily given to some by the masses with the expectation of their welfare as a result. *Government* is the right of commanding given to leaders specifically for the advantages of the governed. Political leaders should be defenders of the people, protectors of property, and guardians of the liberty of their subjects. In return the people consent to obey the laws set forth by the governors. Government becomes nothing more than a robber when it uses the powers given to it by the people to make society unhappy. *The empire of religion* is founded on the idea that it has the power to make nations happy. Government and religion are reasonable institutions, but only to the extent that they contribute to the felicity of the human race. It would be silly to submit to a yoke that results in nothing but evil and misery. It would be complete injustice to force us to renounce our rights without some corresponding advantage!

The authority a father has over his family is based on the idea that he will provide for them. In a political society, rank is based on the real or imaginary usefulness that some citizens offer to others. The former become distinguished citizens and the majority agrees to respect and obey them. The rich acquire rights over the poor by virtue of the welfare they can provide for them. Genius, talents, science, and arts have rights over citizens only as a consequence of the usefulness, happiness, and advantages they provide for society. In a word, it is happiness, or the expectation of it, that we unceasingly imagine and love. Political leaders, corporations, and the wealthy may easily dazzle, intimidate, or impose their will on the society, but they can never earn the voluntary submission of the heart which is the only way to have a legitimate right to rule. For this to happen leaders must display virtue and the people must experience real benefits. Usefulness is nothing more than true happiness. To be useful is to be virtuous, and to be virtuous is to make others happy.

The happiness we experience is the invariable and necessary standard for how we judge the people with whom we associate, the objects we desire, the opinions we embrace, and our actions. We fall victim to our prejudices every time something other than this standard guides our judgment. We will never deceive ourselves if we look closely at how religion, superstition, laws, institutions, inventions, and the various actions of all mankind affect our species. And if we are seduced by a superficial promise of happiness, experience aided by reflection will guide us back to reason which will never deceive. We will learn that pleasure is momentary happiness which frequently becomes an evil, and that evil is temporary trouble that frequently becomes a good. We grow to understand the true nature of objects which enable us to foresee the effects we should expect. We become capable of distinguishing between the desires that are beneficial to our welfare and those seductions that we should resist. We will be convinced that the true interests of intelligent beings who love happiness and want to live in that mode is to root out all phantoms, eliminate superstitious ideas, and destroy all prejudices that denigrate virtue and obstruct happiness in this world.

If we look to experience we will see that illusions and false opinions which have become sacred over time are the source of many evils which overwhelm mankind almost everywhere. Due to our ignorance of natural causes we create imaginary causes. When we do not understand how something works or why some things happen we resort to faith in imaginary beings. The threat of eternal punishment makes these imaginary causes fatal ideas that haunt us without making us better people. We tremble without benefit to ourselves or others. Our minds are filled with superstitious ideas that defy reason and prevent us from seeking after our own happiness. Our fears make us slaves to those who deceive us under the pretense of caring about our welfare. We commit acts of evil because we are persuaded that our Gods demand sacrifices. We live in poverty because we are taught that these Gods want us to be miserable in this life. We become slaves to beings created by our own imagination and we never dare to break the chains that bind us. The artful priest and ministers of these divinities lead us to believe that stupidity, the renunciation of reason, idleness of the mind, and despair of the soul, are the surest means of obtaining eternal happiness.

Prejudices, just as dangerous, have blinded us about the true nature of government. In many cases nations are ignorant of the true foundations of authority. And out of fear or ignorance or both people dare not demand happiness from those leaders whose job it is to procure it for them. As a consequence, politics almost everywhere has degenerated into the fatal art of sacrificing the interests of the majority and providing for those of a few privileged irrational beings. In spite of the evils that assault them, nations follow the leaders they have allowed to rule them, foolishly respecting the instruments of their misery. They show a stupid veneration for those who continuously injure them, obeying their unjust will, giving their blood, money, and lives to satisfy the never ending wants of these leaders. They put their happiness in the hands of individuals who, due to their vices and lack of virtue, are not capable of making themselves happy. Under such leadership the physical and moral happiness of the majority are neglected or even annihilated.

The same blindness can be seen in the science of morals. Superstition, which never had anything but ignorance as its foundation and a chaotic imagination as its guide, does not base ethics on our nature or our relationships or the duties that come about as a result of our relations. Instead, in unison with itself, it bases ethics on imaginary relationships which it pretends exist between humans and the invisible powers it so gratuitously imagines. The will of the Divinity was, and still is, communicated to priests via oracles or dreams or the bible, who then communicates His will to the people. These messages frequently make mortals tremble with fear resulting in misery and the most irrational of actions. Out of fear of eternal damnation beings prostrate themselves before these priests who only promise forgiveness at a cost. So, superstition, instead of providing a sure and natural basis for morals gives a shaky foundation at best by demanding ideal duties and acceptance of ideas which are impossible to accurately understand. In other words, superstition first corrupted us, and then penances performed to atone for our actions finished the job by ruining us. When superstition tries to combat our unruly passions it is unsuccessful. Always enthusiastic but lacking experience it has no clue about true solutions. Those it passes as divine remedies are disgusting and only suitable to make people revolt against them. They are ineffective because fantasies cannot control our basic passions to which more real and powerful motives give birth and our nature constantly move us toward. The voice of superstition, or the Gods, could not be heard amidst the confusion of society. Still the religious leaders cry out to us that we cannot be happy without injuring our fellow beings, who are at fault for having different opinions. These vain cries make virtue hateful because it is viewed as an enemy to happiness and the curse of human pleasure. We are never able to perform our real duties because real motives are never presented which would show us a true path where the present is more important than the future, the visible more important than the invisible, and the known more important than the unknown. We became wicked because everything taught us that we must be that way in order to be happy, after which we sighed.

So, the sum of human misery grows due to our superstitions, our governments, our education, our opinions, and the institutions we accept with the belief they will make life more pleasant. Most people are influenced by many, if not all, of the aforementioned flaws simultaneously, which is why so many people are so very confused. It cannot be repeated too frequently, *it is in error that we will find the true spring of those evils with which the human race is afflicted*. It is not nature that makes us miserable. It is not an irritated Divinity who wants us to live in tears. It is not heredity that causes us to be wicked. It is error, long cherished consecrated error, error which is part of our very existence, to which these terrible effects can be attributed.

The goodness that philosophers seek and that others try to teach with great passion may be considered unrealistic, like a panacea that has been offered as a universal cure. All humans are diseased, most from birth, when error contaminates the thought process. All are affected differently as a consequence of their natural organization. Is there a universal remedy which will indiscriminately cure our diseases? There is without doubt only

ONE and it is TRUTH which must be drawn from Nature.

When contemplating the troubling errors which blind most mortals or the delusions which we are indoctrinated with from birth or the irregular desires that perpetually disturb us or the physical and moral evils that assault us from every direction, one might be tempted to believe that happiness was not meant for this world. Surely, any attempt to cure minds that everything conspires to poison would be done in vain. Consider the many superstitions that keep us in a continuous state of alarm, dividing us from our fellow beings and making us vindictive, persecuting, and irrational. Add to that the many despotic governments that oppress and torture us with a multitude of contradictory and unintelligible laws. And if we think about the cruel ignorance that takes place all over the planet and the crimes that destroy societies we will see the vices that make life so hateful to almost every individual. It's hard to keep your mind from thinking that misfortune and unhappiness are all that the human species has to look forward to and that happiness is nothing more than a dream or a point so far away that it cannot be reached.

So, superstitious mortals, ill-natured individuals, and lazy human beings, continuously see nature or its creator as infuriated with the human race. To such people, we are the constant object of heaven's wrath because our desires are irritating and we seek happiness not meant for us. Because we always want more than what we have, we were taught to believe that the things we want are an abomination, not in our best interest, and offensive to the Gods. We are told that abstinence is the only answer and that it is wrong to even think about the things we desire most. We are told to ignore our passions with no distinction regarding those that are beneficial to the beings that we live with and those that are harmful. As such, we become insensible and our own worst enemy. We separate ourselves from our fellow creatures, renouncing pleasure and refusing happiness. They want *that we should cease to be a human, that we should become unnatural.* Mortals! What they are saying is, "You were born to be unhappy!" The author of your existence has destined you for misfortune so accept yourself as miserable. Fight those rebellious desires for objects that make you happy and renounce the pleasures that you love. Give up all worldly desires while living in a society that inflames your imagination and makes you sigh as you see benefits you must not enjoy. Repress your innermost feelings and stop any activity that might put an end to your suffering. Suffer, worry, groan, and be shameful! For you this is the true road to happiness.

Blind spiritual leaders who see our natural state as diseased never acknowledge that our desires are necessary and our passions are essential. Telling us it is wrong to love or even desire legitimate pleasures is to deprive us of activity which is vital to society. Teaching us that we are born evil leads us to despise ourselves. Such beliefs stifle the most practical motives that could guide us to virtue. So, superstitious remedies serve as a despicable panacea which, far from curing the evils that break us down, increase them and make us more desperate. Instead of calming our passions it makes them more dangerous, venomous, and incurable. Superstition turns the tools nature gives us, meant to aid in our self-preservation and lead to happiness, into a curse. Extinguishing our passions will not make us happier. But, turning them into proper channels by directing them toward useful objects will be advantageous to individuals and beneficial to societies.

Despite the errors which blind the human race and the extravagance of our superstitions, not to mention the foolishness of our political institutions and our concerns about post-life destiny, there are happy individuals on earth. Occasionally there are leaders who are animated by the noble passion of making their citizens happy and seeing their nations flourish. Such people have elevated minds, placing their glory in encouraging goodness, finding happiness in controlling poverty, and think that supporting virtue is honorable. They recognize that the genius, whose contributions are timeless, deserves the eulogies of posterity and the admiration of fellow-citizens.

Is the poor individual excluded from happiness? Living in poverty may afford advantages that the wealthy envy. The needy person has simple desires that are usually attainable. The affluent and the powerful frequently are in the position of not knowing what they want or desiring objects that they cannot have or that their laziness makes impossible for them to obtain. The pauper is accustomed to work and knows the benefits of hard labor, whereas the wealthy, who never has to sweat, never knows the same feeling. Exercise results in vigor, health, and contentment while laziness makes one sick and disgusted. Need sets all the springs of the soul to work. It is the mother of industry and from its bosom come genius, talents, and goodness to which the wealthy must pay homage. The poor individual is like a flexible reed who bends without breaking when confronted with the blows of fate, while the storms of adversity tear the rich, like a sturdy oak in the forest, up by the roots.

So, Nature is not cruel to most of her children. The person who is born into obscurity does not know the ambition that devours the leeches of society. They are not familiar with a restlessness that disturbs sleep and are strangers to remorse. They do not know disgust and are unaware of the weariness of those who have everything but don't know how to use their affluence to make themselves or others happy. The more the body works the more the imagination calms itself. The variety of objects they come into contact with kindles the imagination, yet too many objects cause confusion and disgust. The imagination of the poor is focused on necessity. This person has fewer ideas and is acquainted with fewer objects, so consequently desires less and is usually content. On the other hand, all of nature cannot satisfy the imaginary desires of the individual plunged into luxury, who has used and exhausted all common objects. The lower and middle class of most societies, who are viewed as unhappy, frequently enjoy advantages and happiness that is much greater than that of those who oppress and despise them, yet it's the former that envy the latter. Limited desires are a real benefit. The person of meager means desires only bread and will obtain it by sweat and hard work. These meals will be eaten with pleasure unless injustice makes them taste bitter. Indeed, frequently the actions of leaders make millions of people unhappy, sometimes with and sometimes without advantages to the ruler. The excess of oppression sometimes forces people to revolt against the injustices that have been heaped upon them. Injustice reduces poverty to despair making it look to crime as a resource against its misery. An unjust government creates discouraged souls and its actions depopulate a country. The misery of people produces revolutions when minds get to a state of fermentation. The overthrow of an empire is the necessary effect. So, *physics* and *morals* are always connected, or actually the *same thing*.

Even when the bad morals of leaders do not produce such dramatic results, they do generate laziness which fills society with vagrants and scoundrels whose actions are unaffected by superstition or fear of the law. Nothing can make them want to remain an unhappy spectator of welfare which they are not permitted to partake. They seek fleeting happiness, even at the cost of their lives, when injustice does not allow them to earn an honest living, a path that would have made them honest and useful citizens.

Of course, no government can make its entire population happy but it can and should be dedicated to serving the real needs of the majority. A society is as happy as it can be whenever a greater number of its people are fed, clothed, and housed. That is, they can, without an excess of work, provide the wants that nature has made necessary for their existence. Their minds are contented when they know that no power will take from them the fruits of their labor, that they are working for themselves, and that they sweat for the immediate welfare of their families. Unfortunately, there are whole nations where the masses are forced to work, wasting their strength and drenching the earth with their tears in order to maintain the luxury, gratify the whims, and support the corruption of a small number of irrational and useless beings. For this select few happiness has become impossible because their bewildered imaginations no longer know any bounds. This is how superstition and political errors have changed the fair face of nature into a valley of tears.

Because we have not been able to consult reason or know the value of virtue or learn about our true interests or understand how to achieve real happiness, people at the top and the bottom of nations are frequently far from being content. Yet the human race is made up of a greater number of benefits than of evils. Although no one is entirely happy, most find happiness in certain aspect of their lives. Even the person who complains the most wants to live, sometimes for reasons of which the unhappy individual is not even aware. Habits make our troubles seem more bearable. Suspended grief becomes true enjoyment, wants become pleasures when satisfied, and freedom from humiliation and absence of disease are all happy states that we enjoy without even knowing it. Hope, which we almost always have, gets us through the cruelest disasters. The prisoner laughs while in jail and the weary worker sings on the way home. Even those who believe they are the most unfortunate never see death without alarm unless despair has totally disfigured nature in their eyes. So, as long as we want to live, we cannot be thought of as completely unhappy. As long as we have hope we have a great benefit. If we were able to honestly count our pleasures and our pains we would find that the sum of the first is greater than the last. We would also see that we keep a very exact account of the evils but an unfaithful journal of the good. Indeed, we would see that we have very few days that are entirely unhappy over the course of our existence. Our occasional wants result in pleasure when satisfied. The soul is continuously moved by thousands of objects which, through their variety, range, and novelty make us happy. If our evil actions are violent they will not last long and will quickly bring about our demise. When the sorrows of the mind are very powerful, they will move us toward death. When nature presents nothing but unhappiness, at the same time she opens the door to quit life. Do we take it or refuse to enter because we still find pleasure in existence? Are nations reduced to despair and complete misery? If they have the means, and their choices are perish or suffer, they will always make the most violent efforts to extend life and end their suffering.

Because so many people cling to life, it cannot be concluded that we are unhappy. It is an exaggerated view of the evils of mankind that convince us that there is no remedy. Disasters will diminish in proportion to the number of errors we can eliminate from our collective thinking. We must stop thinking that because we continuously form new desires, many of which are difficult or impossible to fulfill, we are infected. As long as we require daily nourishment we should conclude that the body is sound and fulfilling its functions. As long as we have desires the proper deduction should be that the mind is maintaining a necessary amount of activity. From all this we should know that our passions are essential to the happiness of beings who feel, indispensable to those who think, and required to furnish us with ideas. Indeed, they are vital to a creature that must necessarily love and desire the things that contribute to comfort and promise a mode of existence that matches ones energies. As long as we live and have vitality the soul desires. As long as we desire we experience activity which is necessary. As long as we remain active we continue to live. Human life may be compared to a river where waters meet and push each other forward, flowing on without interruption. The waters must flow over a bed that is not of their choosing, encountering obstacles that prevent stagnation. It never stops undulating and sometimes recoils; only to rush forward again continuing with more or less velocity until it is restored to the ocean of nature.

Chapter 17

Remedies For Our Evils; Recapitulation

Whenever we fail to use experiences as a guide we fall into error. Our errors become even more dangerous, assuming a more determined corruption, when they are clothed with the sanction of superstition. At this point we hardly ever return to the paths of truth. We believe ourselves to be deeply interested in ignoring those things that nature puts before us, and fancy the idea that it is to our advantage to not try to understand ourselves. We think that in the interest of our happiness we must shut our eyes to truth. Most moral philosophers have been wrong about the essence of humanity because they deceived themselves about its diseases, they miscalculated suitable cures, and they administered ineffective or even dangerous remedies. All because they have abandoned nature by resisting experience, not consulting reason and ignoring the evidence of their senses. Instead, they followed the impulses of their imaginations which left them either dazzled by enthusiasm or disturbed by fear. Why were they so easily misled? It is so because they preferred the illusions that were believed instead of the realities of nature, *which never deceives*.

An intelligent being is always working toward conservation, real or fictitious interests, and permanent or fleeting welfare. In other words, we are always working toward what we perceive to be our happiness. We fail to understand that desires are natural and passions essential, and that both are necessary emotions that feed the soul. Instead we suppose supernatural causes due to our lack of understanding and try to fix our evils with either useless or dangerous remedies. In an attempt to suppress desires, combat inclinations, and annihilate passions, our spiritual leaders give us useless instructions that are both vague and unrealistic. These vain lessons have influenced no one. At most they have restrained a few timid mortals who are not inclined to evil. More likely they have terrorized those who are more moderate in their nature, and never had any influence over those who are strongly controlled by their passions or habits. The promises of superstition and its dangers creates fanatics and enthusiast, who themselves are either useless or dangerous to society. It never makes us truly virtuous, that is to say, useful to our fellow creatures.

These theories, guided by blind routine, never acknowledge that we must feel, desire, have passions, and satisfy each in proportion to the amount of energy the body and mind provide. We never perceived that education, habit, government, public opinion, and experience would work together to destroy our passions, plunging us into despair and providing remedies that are too revolting for our temperament. In an affluent society where we know by experience that wealth procures pleasure, we are told it is wrong to desire riches or make any effort to obtain them. To tell us that we must detach ourselves from them is to tell us that we must be miserable. To tell an ambitious individual that that it is wrong to covet power is to order that person to ignore the habitual system of formed ideas. To tell us that passions for objects we desire must be stifled is to require us to renounce happiness. Using superstition to control such practical and powerful interests is to fight realities with fanciful speculations.

If we were to examine, without prejudice, the principles taught by superstition we would see that they were given to us by mortals who say the source is supernatural. As such, their fanatical dogmas are presented as fact. With the slightest reflection it would be obvious that these principles are as ridiculous as they are impossible to put into practice. To prohibit passions is to tell us that we cannot be human creatures. To tell a person with an active imagination to moderate desires is to require a change in temperament. To tell us to renounce our habits is like telling a man who is used to wearing clothes that he must walk around naked. The remedies superstition puts forth to address our depravities are the equivalent of asking a woman to change the configuration of her face or extinguish her imagination or command her not to have passions that excite action within her. They require us to change habits that have been formed over a lifetime of causes and effects and have been converted into wants. Is it surprising that they do not produce the desired effects and only reduce us to a state of despair caused by the continual conflict between passions of the heart and fanciful doctrines? We also experience conflicts between our vices, our virtues, our habits, and those chimerical fears with which superstition constantly overwhelms us. We are drawn to one side by the pleasures we see and experience within a society, as well as the benefits that education, example, and public opinion solidify as desirable. On the other side we are confronted with a gloomy morality that is based on superstitious illusions that solicit us in vain. So, superstition plunges us into misery, creating a violent inner struggle with the heart where there can be no winner. When, by accident, the heart does prevail against so many united forces, it leaves us unhappy, completely destroying the spring of the soul.

Since passions are the true counterbalance to passions, there should be no attempt to destroy them. Instead they should be directed so there is a balance between prejudicial and useful passions. *Reason*, the fruit of experience, is the art of choosing the passions that will lead to each individual's unique form of happiness. *Education* is the art of distributing proper methods of cultivating advantageous passions in our hearts. *Legislation* is the art of restraining dangerous passions while exciting those which may be conducive to public welfare. *Superstition* is the miserable art of planting unproductive labor by nourishing the soul with chimeras, illusions, impostures, and uncertainties, from which passions arise that are fatal to all who fall victim to them. It is only by facing superstitions with fortitude that one can place ones-self on the road to happiness. *True religion is the art of advocating for truth, renouncing error, contemplating reality, drawing wisdom from experience, and cultivating nature to our happiness by teaching the importance of helping others.* It is *reason, education,* and *legislation* that work together to improve human existence by causing our passions to flow in a current, gently creating personal happiness.

Reason and *morals* are useless if they do not point out to each individual that one's conduct is beneficial only if it helps ones-self and others. For a person's conduct to be useful it must help the individual gain the favor of the beings that are necessary for personal happiness. So, in the interest of mankind, which is for the happiness of the human race, early education should teach the importance of self-esteem, love for fellow beings, and the advantages of both. Education should positively stimulate the imagination of each citizen. This is the true means of getting those happy results that habits will make familiar, that public opinion will honor, and that example will continuously direct us toward. *Government* should recognize those who follow the plan and punish those who interrupt it. The hope of true welfare and the fear of real evil will be passions strong enough to deter those that might be harmful to society. Such people will be rare when, instead of feeding our mind with unintelligible speculations and words that make no sense, we are taught only realities and shown only those things that are in unison with truth.

We are frequently wicked because we think it is in our best interest to be that way. We will be happier and better when we are more enlightened, more familiar with truth, and more accustomed to virtue. A government that is equitable and vigilant will fill a society with honest citizens by showing them reasons for goodness, the advantages of truth, and real motives to be virtuous. By instructing people in their duties and fostering them with its goals, government will allure us with the promise of happiness for each individual. When such promises are faithfully fulfilled, the effect will be far more powerful than those of a gloomy superstition, which never promises anything more than imagined benefits and false punishments that the wicked individual never believes if there is the slightest motivation to ignore them. Present motives are always far more effective than those that are distant and at best uncertain. There are so many wicked and vicious people on this planet because there are so few governments that make people feel the advantages of being just, honest, and happy. Instead, in most places, the interest of the powerful invite the common citizens to criminal behavior by favoring the inclinations of a vicious government and by tolerating desires which nothing has tried to control or lead to virtue. A savage who does not know the value of money would not commit a crime to obtain it if transplanted into a civilized society. He would learn to desire it and make an effort to obtain it, and if he could do so without danger he would steal it, especially if he had never been taught to respect the property of others. The savage and the child are in exactly the same state. It is the negligence of society, of those entrusted with their education that makes both wicked. The son of a leader learns to desire power from infancy and becomes ambitious at an early age. As he gains power he may become wicked if he knows he can get away with it. So, it is not nature that makes us wicked but our institutions which direct us to vice. The infant brought up among robbers will most likely learn to steal, while if raised by honest people would probably be virtuous.

If the source of our profound ignorance with respect to morals were to be traced, that is the motives that can give desire to the will, it would be found in the false ideas that so many have formed about human nature. The science of morals has become a puzzle that is impossible to solve because we have made ourselves double by distinguishing the soul from the body. We also think that the nature of the soul is different from that of all known beings. We have given it modes of action and properties distinct from all other bodies. We have emancipated the soul from physical laws so we could submit it to whimsical laws that are enforced in imaginary places at very remote and distant locations. Religious and political leaders have used these gratuitous suppositions, refining and redefining them until they have become completely unintelligible. These moralists do not see that motion is as essential to the soul as it is to a living body and that both are moved by material, physical, objects. Both work unceasingly to regenerate themselves. The wants of the soul as well as the body are purely physical. But, they don't want you to believe that both are intimately and constantly connected or allow that they are both the same under different points of view. Obstinate in their supernatural and unintelligible opinions, they refuse to open their eyes which would convince them that when the body suffers so does the soul and visa versa. Both the pleasures and agonies of the mind affect the body, making it either lazy or active. Instead they have chosen to believe that the soul draws its thoughts, whether pleasant or gloomy, from its own peculiar sources. In fact, it only derives its ideas from material objects that strike the physical organs. It is happy or sad due to the actual state, be it permanent or transitory, of the fluids and solids that make up the body. They have been unwilling to acknowledge that the soul is purely passive and undergoes the same changes as the body. It is acted on by outside objects, frequently without realizing it and often in spite of itself, which interact with the senses and result in sensations, perceptions, and ideas that make it either happy or unhappy.

As a consequence of these opinions, combined with marvelous systems or systems invented to justify them, they have declared the soul to be a free agent. They have given it the ability to move itself and act independent of impulses received from exterior object through organs of the body. They go as far as to say that it can even resist outside impulses and move by its own energies. Yet they insist that it is not different than other beings in nature, it just has a separate mode of action. In other words, it's an isolated point which is not part of the uninterrupted chain of motion whereby bodies communicate to each other in nature and whose parts are always in action. Smitten with their sublime notions, these speculators were not aware that by distinguishing the soul from the body and from all known beings, they make it impossible to form any true idea about it. They are unwilling to see the perfect analogy between the actions of the soul and how they affect the body. They shut their eyes to the necessary and continual correspondences that exist between the soul and the body. They do not perceive that the soul, like the body, is subject to the motion of attraction and repulsion, which give it physical qualities that act upon the organs of the body. The activity of the will, the passions, and the continual regeneration of its desires are never more than consequences of activity produced in the body by material objects, which it has no control over. These object make it miserable or happy, active or lazy, contented or discontented, and all in spite of itself. No matter how clear these facts may be, they choose to look to the heavens for unknown powers to set the soul in motion. They hold forth distant, imaginary interests under the pretext of procuring future happiness for us. Instead they keep us from working toward our happiness and increasing our knowledge as we look to the heavens and lose sight of the earth. We have not been told the truth and are lead to believe not knowing it will make us happy. But that happiness is always an immense distance away, while our life on earth is filled with terrors, shadows that we can never come into contact with, and chimeras formed by our bewildered imaginations, which change as often as the government to which we submit. So, hoodwinked by our fears and blinded by our gullibility, *we are guided through the meandering path of life by people who are as blinded as we are, where both one and the other are frequently lost in the maze.*

Conclusion

From everything that has been said up to this point, it is clear that the errors of mankind, whatever they may be, arise because we ignore reason, experience, and the evidence the senses provide. Instead we allow our misguided imaginations and suspicious authority figures to direct us. We will never find true happiness as long as we refuse to study nature and her laws. We must look to her alone for solutions to the evils that result from so many errors. We will be a mystery to ourselves as long as we ignore the laws of nature and believe ourselves to be two beings, one of which is moved by an inconceivable spiritual power. If we do not see our moral and intellectual faculties in the same way we see our physical qualities, they will always be a mystery. We must recognize that they are governed by the same regulations and submit to the same impulses as everything in nature. The idea that we are a free agent is contradicted at every instant by experience which proves that all our actions are necessary. This truth, far from being dangerous and destructive to our morals, gives us the insight to see why relationships must exist between sensible beings within a society. People congregate with a view of uniting their efforts for the happiness of all. From these necessary relationships come the duties that must be performed to coexist. As such, we will learn the sentiment of love which should be associated with virtuous conduct, while rejecting all that is vicious and criminal. All this will make the true foundation of *Moral Obligation* obvious, which is figuring out how to get what we want the most as a result of uniting in society. Each individual can tend to personal interests, happiness, and security by contributing to the needs, happiness, and preservation of associates and the community. It's about the necessary actions and re-actions of the human will on the necessary attraction and repulsion of our soul, upon which all our morals are grounded. It's the harmony of the will and the performance of our actions that maintains society. It is made miserable by conflicts and dissolved through a lack of unity.

From all that has been said, it can be concluded that the many names we have given to the concealed causes acting in nature, and their various effects, are never more than *necessity* considered under different points of view. It must also be acknowledged that the original cause, the great *cause of causes*, is something of which we will always be ignorant. What we call *order* is a necessary consequences of causes and effects that we understand, or think we understand, and that we find pleasing and conformable to our existence. Similarly what we call *confusion* is a consequence of necessary causes and effects, which we do not understand and therefore views as unfavorable or unsuitable. A few we have designated as:

Intelligence – our ability to understand necessary causes that necessarily operate the chain of events which we call *order*.
Divinity – those invisible causes which act in nature according to immutable and necessary laws.
Destiny or fatality – the necessary connection between unknown causes and effects seen in the world.
Chance – those effects which we are not able to foresee or which we are ignorant of the necessary connection with their causes.
Intellectual and moral faculties – those effects and those changes necessary to an organized being whom we think is moved by an inconceivable agent and who we believe is distinguished from the body. It has a nature totally different from the body which we call the SOUL. We believe this agent is immortal unlike the body. It has been shown that the marvelous doctrine of another life is based on gratuitous beliefs, contradicted by reflection, unsupported by experience, and may or may not be true. Mortals know nothing about the subject. It has been proven that the hypothesis of another life is not only useless to our morals, but it is calculated to stop us from actively pursuing the road to true happiness. Instead it fills us with romantic ideas that inebriate us with opinions that work against our tranquility. It takes the focus of legislators away from education, institutions, and the laws of society, all of which should be their true interests and duties.

Politics has repeatedly adopted wrong opinions based on ideas that are not capable of satisfying the passions that everything conspires to kindle in the heart. We stop looking to the future as the present seduces us and hurries us along. It has been shown that fear of death is an advantageous sentiment because it motivates us to actions that may be truly useful to society. From all this, it is obvious what is necessary to lead us to happiness and how error provides obstacles to oppose it.

We cannot try to defeat prejudice without enlightening the mind, or combat error without substituting truth, or underrate the great *cause of causes*, or address the foundations of superstition and those of morals at the same time. The last is necessary because it is based on our nature. Its duties are certain and must last as long as the human race remains. It imposes obligations on humans because without it neither individuals nor societies can exist and obtain or enjoy the advantages that nature requires us to desire.

Mankind! Listen to the morals which are based on experience and grounded on the necessity of things. Ignore superstitions that are founded on musings, deception, and the unpredictable whims of disordered imaginations. Instead, follow the lessons of those humane and gentle morals which conduct us to virtue through the voice of happiness. Turn a deaf ear to the useless cries of superstition which really make us unhappy, while making truth hateful and painting veracity in hideous colors, never leading us to respect VIRTUE. See if REASON, without the assistance of a rival who prohibits its use, will conduct us toward that great end which is the object of our research and the natural tendency of all our views.

Indeed, up to now what benefits has the human race drawn from those sublime supernatural notions which superstition has fed mortals for so many ages? Nothing but phantoms created by ignorance and enhanced by active imaginations. We've been told to believe so many subtle and irrational theories that use words devoid of meaning and from which experience is forbidden. Fantastical hopes and panic terrors have been used to influence our will. And what have they done? Have any of them made us better, enlightening us as to what we must do, and help us perform those actions better? Have any of the marvelous systems and the inventions that support them resulted in conviction of the mind, reasoned conduct, or a more virtuous heart? Have they led us in any way to understanding the great *Cause of Causes*? Alas, it is a sad fact that cannot be repeated frequently enough that all these things have done nothing more than plunge human understanding into a darkness from which it is difficult to withdraw. They have sown into our hearts the most dangerous of errors from which it is almost impossible to divert. They have given birth to those fatal passions which are the true source of the evils that have tormented our species without ever enlightening our minds with truth or leading to a healthy worship, which we do best through a rational enjoyment of the faculties with which we are gifted.

For the unfortunate beings that live in continuous contradiction with themselves, never finding inner peace or the ability to conform within a society, whatever your crimes and whatever your fears of punishments in another life are, aren't you already cruelly punished in this life? Don't your own excesses and shameful habits result in poor health, disgust, and fatigue? Don't your vices dig your grave as you live everyday with the knowledge of your actions? Don't you tremble with the fear that you may be caught, or worse that you have to see a person with so many problems every time you look in the mirror? You should not fear death as it will put an end to the torments you have inflicted on yourself. *Death, in delivering from the earth a troublesome birth, will also deliver you from your most cruel enemy, yourself.*

O mortal, stop allowing yourself to be disturbed by illusions and phantoms that were created by your own imagination or that of some cunning imposture. Renounce your vague hopes and disengage from your overwhelming fears so you can follow with confidence the necessary routine that nature has marked out for you. Cover your path with flowers if destiny permits and remove the thorns that cover it if you can. Don't attempt to focus your views on a murky future whose obscurity ought to be enough to prove that it is either dangerous or useless to try to understand. Concentrate on making yourself happy in your existence. Be moderate and reasonable when it comes to your self-preservation. Balance your pleasures and avoid anything that can be harmful to you or others. Be truly intelligent by learning self-esteem so that you can preserve yourself and reach your highest goals at every moment of your existence. Be virtuous in order to make yourself solidly happy so that you can secure the esteem, enjoy the affections, and benefit from the assistance of those who surround you, which are those beings that nature has made necessary to your existence and happiness. And even when those who surround you are unjust, make yourself worthy of their admiration and your own self-love and you will live a content, serene, and remorse free life. For you, death will be a door to a new existence, a new order that you will be submitted to which is controlled by the eternal laws of nature, which maintains that to LIVE HAPPY HERE, YOU MUST MAKE OTHERS HAPPY. Allow yourself to be drawn gently along your journey until you return to that peaceable sleep on the bosom that gave birth to you. And if, contrary to my expectations, there is another life of eternal happiness you will surely be allowed to partake.

End of Volume

www.ingramcontent.com/pod-product-compliance
Lightning Source LLC
Chambersburg PA
CBHW071431070526
44578CB00001B/69